305.244   Marston, Stephanie.
MAR
         If not now, when?

$22.95

Ventress Memorial Library
Library Plaza
Marshfield, MA 02050

BAKER & TAYLOR

If Not Now, When?

Reclaiming Ourselves at Midlife

Stephanie Marston

WARNER BOOKS

A Time Warner Company

I Dedicate This Book
to the Memory of My Mother,
Selma Small.
I Love, Appreciate, and Miss You More Than
Words Can Express.
And to My Daughter,
Ama Marston, Who Is Carrying the Torch Magnificently.

Contents

Acknowledgments

No book is written alone. Inevitably, there are people who offer essential support and encouragement along the way. First, I would like to thank the women who took the time and so generously shared their stories with me. Without you, this book would not exist. Thanks to the members of Virginia Satir's Avanta Network who facilitated my contact with many of these women.

To my adopted family, Cathy and Dan Warren, my soul sister Georgia Noble, Anne Scholder, Bonnie Solow, Valerie and Joe Bechtol, Herb and Evy Weinstein, and Joan Glasser. It's true that home is where the heart is.

To Celeste Fremon, my dear friend and "ideal reader," whose support and feedback was invaluable in shaping this book. Thanks for being there through it all.

It takes a special man to be able to work on a book about women, let alone women and midlife. My writing coach, Kit Rachlis, is just such a man. Your insightful editing, expertise, reassurance, and steadfastness have not only made me a better writer but this a better book. Kit, thanks for being such a mensch.

To Carol Trussell for taking the time to read the finished manuscript and for giving me your thoughtful comments.

To Dorothy Kraft, a lifelong friend, mentor, and inspiration. You fostered my embryonic talents well before I knew they existed. You were a safe harbor when I needed one. For this and so much more, I am eternally grateful.

To Bea Cooper, who continues to offer support and sage counsel even from afar.

There are some doctors, health practitioners, and instructors who are worth their weight in gold. I am fortunate to have Dr. Karen Blanchard, Lisa Wilson, and Gail Ackerman on my team.

To my sister, Marian Small, for being my partner in fighting the "evil empire."

To Richard Rubin, Cassondra Joseph, Jean and Charlie Segal, Sarah and Jack Doppelt, and Marge Karpas, without whom I wouldn't have made it through one of the more difficult situations of my life.

To Patty Aubery for sharing her marketing genius and expertise with me. You taught me about a whole other reality.

To Jack Canfield for your ongoing support and generosity.

To the staff of Chicken Soup for the Soul, thanks for all your help.

The work of Gail Sheehy, Terri Apter, and Carol Gilligan has been extremely valuable in shaping my early ideas for this book. Thank you for your pioneering work.

Many thanks to the staff at the Santa Fe Public Library

reference desk for your willingness to look up all manner of trivia and for hunting down countless obscure facts.

To my agent, Loretta Barrett, who believed in this project from its inception and whose advice and guidance I value tremendously. To Jamie Raab at Warner Books for acquiring this book. Thanks for your understanding, patience, and support. To my editor, Claire Zion, who has been a cheerleader and astute reader. Your enthusiasm and genuine love of the material have meant a great deal to me. You are truly a kindred spirit. To Maggie Crawford, who inherited this project and helped usher it into the world. To Michele Bidelspach, thanks for taking care of all the details.

To my daughter, Ama, you are an inspiration and light in my life. Thanks for all the love and wackiness.

If Not Now, When?

If I am not for myself, who is for me?
If I am only for myself, what am I?
And if not now, when?

—HILLEL

Prologue

It was a hot summer afternoon. I had gone to a yoga class. For the first time all year, I could shed my black tights and sweatshirt for shorts and a skimpy T-shirt. I was struggling to get into a pose, when I suddenly caught a glimpse of a woman in the floor-to-ceiling mirror. I immediately noticed that she no longer had salt-and-pepper hair. It was now mostly salt. The skin on her thighs gathered about her knees like crepe paper. Although she had never been described as voluptuous, her breasts now seemed to be missing in action. Who was that? This couldn't be me. Sure, I'd noticed myself aging as I looked in the bathroom mirror, but I'd never taken it all in.

It wasn't just the physical changes that made me unrecognizable to myself but a shift in attitude, as well. Everyone in the class, including all the other women, was doing a supported handstand. I, however, had decided to sit this one out. In the past, I would have pushed myself. I would have been unable to tolerate feeling less capable.

Yet I realized that with the amount of time I spent at the computer, it wasn't worth the additional stress on my wrists. As I stood there, I experienced a new sense of vulnerability—a vague sadness engulfed me. I thought, My God, somehow while I wasn't paying attention, I've gotten older.

It wasn't just that I wasn't turning heads anymore that bothered me. It was also that I felt different—as if I'd let go of something familiar and comfortable. In fact, I no longer felt like the person I'd been. But I wasn't sure who this new me was. I knew intellectually that this change was not only necessary but also for the better. Still, the reality of the change unsettled me. The vulnerability I was experiencing during yoga signaled something larger. I began to worry. I no longer felt as bold or secure as I had in the past. I was afraid that I might not like this new me as much as the old one. Would she be as valued or as effective as my earlier self?

As if that weren't enough, this profound realization that I'd gotten older occurred at about the same time that my mother died. My entire world went tilt. After my mother's death, everything I'd clung to and thought was important came into question. Who am I really? What do I believe in? What's truly important? What is it I want out of life? As I mulled over these questions, I began to realize just how much of my life had been motivated by proving myself, by pleasing my parents, lovers, husband, child, friends, siblings. I knew that my motivation had to change. For all of the therapy I'd done, for all the clients I'd counseled, the books I'd written, the confident face I'd presented to the world, it wasn't until I entered midlife that I realized just how disconnected I still was from my essential self. A gap remained between my inner reality and the self I presented to the world. I felt fragmented.

So I decided to see what had been written on women and midlife. But when I went to the bookstore, I couldn't find anything that addressed the issues I was struggling with. Sure, there was a variety of books, but they were primarily about the physical aspects of menopause. Others had snippets about midlife and women. None, though, answered my questions. None focused on the change I felt in relation to my sexuality and appearance, how to integrate aspects of my personality I'd previously neglected, the desire I felt for greater equality in my relationships, how to cope with the dismantling of many of the beliefs upon which I had based my life, the need for more balance between my vulnerability and my strength, or how to incorporate passion and creativity into my everyday life. It was at this point that I began to talk with all the smart middle-aged women I knew in order to find out how they were handling this thing called midlife.

For the past twenty years, my professional passion had been working with children and parents both as a family therapist and seminar leader. However, when my daughter left for college, my interest in parenting diminished and the focus of my private practice shifted. I began to see women in their forties, fifties, and even some in their sixties. As a result of my own quest, as well as my clinical work, midlife became my new preoccupation.

Out of the interactions I had with my clients as well as from the initial conversations with other midlife women, the idea for this book was born. They, too, wanted to hear what other women were experiencing, how they were coping with the challenges and opportunities presented during this time. It was then that I began to facilitate groups for women in midlife. The response I received told me how strong the need truly was. In fact, I often found it difficult to bring the evening to a close. After each session, women would continue the discussion. It was obvious that they found comfort and strength in their shared struggles, experiences, and triumphs.

As a result of these groups, I interviewed more than a hundred women from all walks of life, in a multitude of situations, from across the country. Every woman was interesting in her own way; each woman's story was unique. Yet there were common themes. After each interview, I was elated. I felt as if I'd hit pay dirt. Although the women often faced daunting issues, each was now circling back to reclaim dreams and needs she had lost along the way. What I found, with few exceptions, was that women experience midlife as a time of renewal and rebirth. Some expressed this more tentatively than others, but almost all characterized this as one of the best times of their lives. The depth, strength, resilience, generosity, resourcefulness, and wisdom of these women were inspiring.

My hope is that this book will encourage you to see yourself in the stories of these women—women who have struggled at times, yet successfully navigated this transition. Some of you may just be entering midlife, while others of you are right smack in the middle of it. I think that you'll find that wherever you are in this transition, the issues discussed will be both relevant and stimulating. As you become immersed in these women's stories, I hope that you'll be moved to examine your own quest for greater fulfillment. As you do, I invite you to use this book as a catalyst to talk with other women about this extraordinary time of life. While there are no maps to this journey, this book can act as a companion to provide the reassurance and understanding that can help you make this passage meaningful and transformative.

Chapter 1

THE CALL OF THE AUTHENTIC SELF

As life goes on it becomes tiring to keep up the character you invented for yourself, and so you relapse into individuality and become more like yourself every day. This is sometimes disconcerting for those around you, but a great relief to the person concerned.

—AGATHA CHRISTIE

It is never too late to be what you might have been.

—GEORGE ELIOT

Hail pelted my office window as Linda dashed in from the afternoon thunderstorm. She was dressed in an elegant suit, matching heels, and a periwinkle scarf. As she settled onto the couch, she held herself stiffly and seemed uneasy. Her short blond hair was tinged with gray, and there was only a trace of lipstick left on her thin, dry lips. There were dark circles under her eyes. Fifty years old, Linda had been married to her second husband for twelve years. She had two children from her first marriage, both of whom were in college, and a stepdaughter, who was a senior in high school. Linda was the chief human resources officer at a national bank. She had a good marriage, a thriving career, and her children were flourishing. But despite all of her success, her voice sounded flat, and there was a deadness in her eyes.

I asked Linda what had brought her to see me. "Actually, I'm a bit embarrassed," she said. "I love my husband, I have great kids, and my career is going well. But lately I just feel like I'm stalled. I have more success than I ever could have imagined. I know I should be happy, but I have this unsettling feeling that something's missing. But I don't know what it is. I just walk around with this hollowness in the pit of my stomach. Except for my divorce, I've pretty much played by the rules of what a girl from Baton Rouge was expected to do. I went to college right after high school, got married, had my children in my twenties, and went into the corporate world, where I've done very well."

I asked Linda what felt empty. She sat silently for a moment. "So much of my life has revolved around my career," she said, letting out a sigh. "My job is incredibly demanding. I work in my car; I work at the office. My husband teases me about how my side of the bed looks more like a command center than a place to relax."

Linda had just been offered a promotion. While she would have jumped at the opportunity a year or two ago, she now felt conflicted and uncertain. "I should be thrilled," she said. Instead, she was having trouble sleeping and was plagued by anxiety. "We could really use the additional income, especially since we'll have another kid in college. But I just don't know if I can do it. No, let me correct that. I don't know if I *want* to do it. This is so unlike me. I usually do what's in front of me, but for some reason, I can't now. I'm afraid of doing something different. But I'm more afraid not to."

As I listened to Linda, I heard echoes of the voices of many of the women I have worked with in my private practice. So many had experienced a period of intense questioning during midlife. I reassured Linda that she was not alone in her struggle. Dissatisfaction and self-examination are essential to navigating this passage of life successfully. After all, midlife is a time of tremendous change for women. Our ability to conceive and bear children comes to an end. We become less visible in our culture. And often we begin to feel an unease with many aspects of our lives, our relationships, our work.

From the vantage point of midlife, we can look back and take stock of where we have been, what we've done, and where we want to go from here. It's not uncommon for a woman to feel that she wants to step free of the scripted life and roles she has been living and search for who she is in the depth of her being.

Like Linda, many of us become impatient with what isn't working. During the first half of our lives, when our focus was on establishing a family and a career, we stifled our own voice, sublimating our needs to attend to those of husband, children, and work. With many of these external structures now in place, we discover that aspects of ourselves, which we had previously rejected, resurface. Midlife is a time when women long for a greater sense of wholeness.

Linda came in a week later. She had just learned that her oldest friend, whom she had known since second grade, had been diagnosed with breast cancer. Although her friend lived one thousand miles away in New Orleans, the two women remained close. They talked on the phone at least once a month. Every summer for the past fifteen years, they had gone on a "Thelma and Louise getaway." As soon as she found out about her friend's illness, Linda went to see her.

Although the cancer had been detected early, it had been found in three lymph nodes. To be on the safe side, the oncologist had recommended that her friend have a mastectomy and begin chemotherapy. "When I arrived, Jen had just returned from the cancer center," Linda said. "She was terrified. She thought that her life might be over. I crawled into bed with her and held her while she cried. When she sat up, there was a clump of hair on the pillow. I didn't know what to do.

"Still, in the midst of all she was going through, Jen hadn't lost her sense of humor. She told me that she'd always wondered what she'd look like as a brunette, and finally she had gotten her chance. She asked me to bring her the wig her mother had bought her. When she put it on, we burst out laughing. 'Admit it. I look like Flip Wilson playing Geraldine on a bad day,' she roared. It was such a relief to see my friend, who was so frail and weak, act as irreverently as ever."

Linda was shaken by her friend's cancer. I could hear in her voice an uncertainty that I hadn't heard in our previous session. Suddenly, her own sense of mortality had become real. The awareness of death distinguishes midlife from other stages of development in a woman's life. Death becomes our adviser and shakes us out of the numbness and complacency that can mark so much of our lives. It can create a sense of urgency—an imperative of grow or die. It can inspire a woman to examine what is most meaningful for her, how she wants to invest her time and energy and enjoy the life that is to come.

Linda could have been speaking for countless other women who undergo a period of profound reevaluation during midlife. Most of us go blithely about our daily preoccupations until a crisis or some vague internal stirring stops us long enough to focus our attention on the need to discover the deeper meaning in our lives. The uncertainty that Linda was experiencing was less about her career than about personal transformation. In her case, it was sparked by her friend's illness. But for other women, it can be triggered by a divorce, a parent's dying, a child's leaving home or needing our involvement far more or far less, a change in work, or a shift in the power balance of a marriage. Regardless of the cause, midlife is a time when we are ripe for significant change.

Since she'd learned of her friend's cancer, Linda had come to realize that having a comfortable home, a nice car, and a prestigious career were enjoyable, but they certainly weren't what was most important. Linda's friend was at the height of her career when doctors discovered the cancer. She had just been featured on the cover of *New Orleans* magazine. Her illness had caused Linda to think about what was most important to her; she realized that more work, longer hours, and increased stress were not what she wanted.

"I just hit the big five oh," Linda said. "It really struck me that time is moving on. I was playing the Bonnie Raitt song,

"Nick of Time." I never listened to the words before, but she said, 'Life gets mighty precious when there's less of it to waste.' I realized how much of my life has been dominated by my work and caring for others. I started to think about my wish list. It was something that Jen actually thought of for her kids. Then she realized she wanted to make one for herself. While her children's list was made up of things they wanted her to buy, ours are about all the things we've dreamed of doing but haven't done."

I asked Linda what were some of the things on her list. "I've always wanted to go on an archaeological dig. Don't ask me why. But it's something I've dreamt about since I took a class in art history in college, about the pre-Hispanic Andes. Before Jen's cancer, I used to think that I had an unlimited amount of time to do the things that are important to me. Not anymore. I don't want to get to the end of my life and be filled with regrets. Really, I wonder what the heck I've been waiting for. There's this phrase that keeps echoing in my mind: If not now, when?"

In interviews with more than one hundred women from across the country, I heard this phrase over and over again. While it was often expressed in different words, they all echoed the same sentiment. One woman said, "It's now or never. Whatever it is I've been wanting in my life, now's the time." Another talked about "living more in the moment and not holding back anymore." Yet another woman expressed it as "not waiting for someone else's permission." Still another woman said, "Whatever I'm going to make of my life or myself, this is the time." In the end, it all came down to "If not now, when?"

Midlife is a time of inner work—a time to bring our lives under our own authority. It's a time when we shift our focus away from the practical concerns of the first half of our lives toward the search for deeper meaning.

Midlife is about remembering. Remembering who we truly are. Remembering our visions, hopes, and dreams. Remembering our deepest yearnings. It's about remembering what we've lost and about reclaiming it. Midlife is a time when we come fully into our own, reclaiming our strength, passion, vitality, wisdom, and compassion. It's a time from which every woman can emerge a new person.

As we question what we have sacrificed in order to be a devoted mother, a wife, a career woman, we also can now unearth the secret wishes that will take us back to our authentic selves. Regardless of whether we're still involved in raising children, midlife is when we bring ourselves back into the picture and begin to attend to our long-neglected or forgotten needs and longings.

Do You Believe It? We're the Grown-ups Now!

For many women of the baby-boom generation, the arrival of midlife is often unsettling. It seems like only yesterday that our parents were the responsible ones—the ones who held positions of power and authority. But you know you're a grown-up when someone says, "Excuse me, ma'am." You look around to see whom they're talking to, only to discover that they're talking to you. You think, Ma'am? Me "ma'am"? They must be kidding. How absurd. I'm no ma'am. Barbara Boxer, Charlayne Hunter-Gault, Donna Shalala—These are women who should be addressed as ma'am. Women of power, authority, responsibility. Women of a certain age. But wait a minute. These women are our age. And the reality sets in that we have crossed the great divide. We're no longer the generation of hope and promise. While many of us feel years younger than the age on our driver's licenses, we aren't kids anymore. We're now the grown-ups, the older generation.

The irony is that while we may look like grown-ups, and even act like them, at least some of the time, in our heart of hearts there lives a free-spirited, raucous girl. There's a part of us that still longs to drive down the coast in a red Mustang convertible with the top down, that would like to turn on the ceiling sprinklers in an overly stuffy business meeting, that wants to have an anchovy pizza delivered to our ex-husband or boss, the way we did in junior high. Admit it, some of you still scream obscenities when you're cut off in traffic, and you don't even feel bad about doing it. You fill your water bottle with wine cooler so you can sneak it into the movies. You call the dentist and feign an illness to get out of your appointment. And they call us grown-ups! Well, we are. Just not all the time. Thank goodness, we don't have to be.

But the torch has been passed. After all, someone has to be the grown-up. Our time has come. Much to our surprise, we *are* prepared to meet the task at hand. If the truth be known, it's not half-bad. Many of us never imagined reaching forty. Forty once seemed ancient. The forties, though, provide a new beginning—a beginning that can lead us to the discovery of who we truly are. Now's the time when we come fully into our own. Most women I interviewed are happier now than when they were in their twenties or thirties. While they'd love to have the body they had then, they wouldn't trade where they are in their lives for anything.

Research conducted with the alumnae of Mills College, a women's college in northern California, corroborates my own findings. In a study of seven hundred women between the ages of twenty-six and eighty, the women who most often described their lives as "first-rate" were those in their fifties. Six years later, when the study was repeated, it was again women in their early fifties who were most fulfilled. The women cited a number of reasons: They were more self-confident and decisive; they felt that they were more their own person; and they had developed greater control over their lives.

This Is Not Our Mother's Midlife

Each generation is shaped by the social climate of its time. Our mothers' identities were formed by World War I and the Great Depression. They were taught that the key to a happy life was marrying a stable man and raising a family. The life of the suburban housewife was the fantasy of young American women. A 1955 *New York Times* article on women college students reported, "Girls feel hopeless, if they haven't a marriage at least in sight by commencement time." The primary goal of our mothers' generation was to be loved, chosen, and financially secure.

If a woman's mission was to maintain a marriage and raise a family, middle age posed a threat to her security; she lost her sex appeal, along with her fertility and, consequently, her power. Midlife threatened the very foundation of women's lives. In order for women to feel positive about midlife, they had to believe that they had something worthwhile to offer beyond their youthful appearance and capacity to bear children, and many of these women didn't. All they could see was loss—waning attractiveness, coping with rebellious teenagers, divorce, widowhood, caring for aging parents, menopause. From that perspective, midlife seemed like the beginning of the end.

Until recently, the idea of a midlife crisis was presumed to be the exclusive domain of men. If women experienced any turmoil at midlife, it was minimized—the result of the empty-nest syndrome, say, or being left for another woman, or menopausal malaise. But since the 1950s, women's expectations and prospects have been profoundly transformed. Women went to college, often chose to postpone marriage and motherhood, entered the workforce, ran for political office, and experimented sexually in a way that only men had previously. Women now include success in career, equality in relationships, and ongoing personal growth as issues central to their lives. In light of this dramatic change, the notion of a midlife crisis is now equally relevant for women.

Baby boomers are the first generation of women who have had control over their reproductive life (both birth control and fertility) and have built their identities on their value not only in relationships but also in the workplace. But while women of the baby-boom generation were prepared for "traditional feminine roles," by the time we came of age, many of us were questioning these conventional values. We wanted to break the mold that had trapped our mothers. While our mothers took pride in being homemakers, we realized that society held them in low esteem. With the overemphasis on women as nurturers and caretakers, their deeper sense of themselves was left acutely underdeveloped. As the daughters of these women, many of us felt compelled to find fulfillment not just within a marriage and family but in the larger world, as well.

Women of the baby boom are better informed and better educated than any previous generation; we've become executives, astronauts, and CEOs of Fortune 500 corporations; we have incomes, not to mention substantial independent incomes; we're more likely to divorce and raise children as a single parent; many of us postponed marriage, remained single, or are in same-sex relationships; and we have fewer children. Former Colorado congresswoman Pat Schroeder put it well when she said, "I have a brain and a uterus, and I use both."

During the 1960s and 1970s, when women of the baby-boom generation became more political, every aspect of our lives came under question. As a result of the civil rights and women's movements, the old gender roles are dead and buried, but no new roles have replaced them. As we have at every point in our lives, we baby-boom women are flying by the seat of our pants.

No, this is not our mother's midlife. Women have worked to expand their identities, from June Cleaver to Hillary Clinton, from Jayne Mansfield to Diane Sawyer. As a result, our lives have grown increasingly complex as well as richer. Baby boomers have redefined marriage, motherhood, childbirth, work, and friendship. So why shouldn't we redefine midlife, as well?

The Crisis: The Call of the Authentic Self

While midlife is a natural stage in a woman's development, there's a good chance that somewhere between the ages of forty and fifty-five, a woman will be shaken to the core of her being. Suddenly, she is thrust into a period of heightened vulnerability—a midlife crisis. Although *crisis* has a negative connotation in our culture, suggesting failure, defectiveness, and weakness, the word is derived from the Greek word *krinein,* or *krisis,* which means "a separating," or "a turning point." The root implies that a crisis is a time of letting go of old ways of being, a time when we can ask ourselves what we need to leave behind and what we can reclaim.

What many women face in midlife is a period of intense reevaluation. We begin to rethink our experiences, relationships, and choices and reconsider what lies ahead. Now we can ask, Who am I really? What do I love? What are my own needs and desires? The choices a woman makes as a result of this reevaluation will resonate throughout the rest of her life. While this crisis can seem overwhelming, it can lead to increased power and a stronger sense of self.

Very often, a woman's sense of self, established in her youth, no longer seems to hold her. The person she had been suddenly feels too confining. It's time to make room for a new adult identity. But this requires that she listen with great care to what is most relevant in her life now and for her future. She must recall the passions and dreams she had abandoned, and nourish the unused aspects of her personality. As in all periods of transition, something must be given up in order for something new to emerge. An author and authority in the field of death and dying, Stephen Levine writes, "Part of me is dying, maybe to let the rest of me come to life." Midlife is a period of chaos and confusion as well as a time of growth, a time from which every woman can emerge a new person.

When a woman realizes that she can no longer rely on the maps she had used during most of her life, she often experiences so much anxiety that she tries to brush aside the changes that are required to make this transition. She may wish to retreat to an earlier phase, in which her self-image and ways of being, though not fulfilling, are familiar at least. Virginia Satir, a pioneer in the field of family therapy, writes, "Most people prefer the certainty of misery to the misery of uncertainty." So it's understandable that a woman may resist the demands of midlife. For most of us, midlife is a journey to an unknown land. We simply don't know what we're going to encounter there. We're desperate to know that things will work out, yet all we can see is the unknown. Whether because our sense of who we are doesn't correspond to our current reality or because we've begun to shed our earlier identity, many of us find ourselves in a state of limbo, feeling as though we've lost our bearings. It's no wonder so many of us resist this transition; midlife requires an immense leap of faith. Almost everything a woman once counted on comes into question, old coping mechanisms no longer work, and we are thrown into a period of psychological upheaval, a genuine identity crisis.

Adolescence: The Sequel

The early stage of midlife is a lot like the transition we go through at adolescence, except we're a lot wiser now. That's some consolation for the fact that where we once spent hours on the phone with our girlfriends talking about making out and dating, now our conversations revolve around which supplements we're taking, how to stop the drenching hot flashes, whether ginkgo will really prevent us from losing our minds, how the print in the newspaper has suddenly gotten infinitesimal, and whether to nip and tuck or not to nip and tuck. The times, they certainly are a-changing.

But just as in adolescence we withdrew from the tasks and attachments of childhood, in midlife we withdraw from the goals and priorities of our first adulthood.

It was only relatively recently that adult development was studied. With the work of psychologists Erik Erikson, Daniel Levinson, Roger Gould, and others, a new way of thinking about human growth was acknowledged by social scientists and psychologists. But most of the research was done by men who wanted to gain insight into their own psychological development. It wasn't until women entered the field of social psychology in large numbers that women's issues were studied. Harvard Professor Carol Gilligan was one of the pioneers in the study of women's development.

In the 1990 book *Making the Connection,* Gilligan discusses how "adolescence is a time of disconnection, sometimes of disassociation or repression in women's lives. [Women] tend to forget or cover over—what as girls they have experienced and known." According to Gilligan, a dramatic change occurs for girls when they enter adolescence. Girls fall asleep to themselves. The self-confident, competent, talented, exuberant, outgoing girl in middle childhood vanishes as she judges herself against an impossible feminine ideal—to please others, to be selfless, nice, pretty, and to make herself the object of someone else's life. To attain that culturally prescribed ideal, a girl stashes away a great many parts of herself. She silences parts of herself. She stops speaking out and expressing her feelings. Instead, she focuses on trying to please others, especially those of the opposite sex.

Adolescence is a time when girls succumb to the cultural riptides that carry them further away from their true selves. As author Mary Pipher observes in her best-selling book, *Reviving Ophelia*, as teenagers, girls desperately want to be accepted. They're faced with an impossible choice: either to remain true to themselves and risk rejection by their friends or to desert their authentic self and be socially acceptable. Unfortunately, the choice for most girls is obvious: to abandon a large part of themselves and sign on for the cruise of acceptability.

Reclaiming Our Authenticity

Midlife is the mirror image of adolescence. Throughout early adulthood, women strive to achieve the ideals they established in adolescence. They need the experience of living before they can confront the limiting accommodations they have made to others' expectations. Many young women sacrificed their gifts and dreams as they left the safety of family and home and entered the larger world, got married, and raised a family. Midlife gives a woman the opportunity to get out, not only from a job but from anything else she may have been doing unquestioningly for a long time.

It's often not until midlife that a woman fully takes possession of her psychological strength and assumes complete responsibility for her own fulfillment. Now that we're no longer dependent on our appearance to define us, now that we are less concerned about other people's opinions, we can recapture the freedom that many women experienced during middle childhood. We reenter a period when we were self-confident, followed our own instincts, and explored our many varied interests. Midlife is a time when women come full circle and reclaim the outspokenness, enthusiasm, adventurousness, and vitality that we once had. Midlife is often a time when we retrieve the girl in jeans, ponytails, and denim shirt from the lost and found.

In speaking to numerous women, both in my private practice as well as during interviews, it was clear that while each woman's longing is unique, there is a universal theme: They all want to be who they truly are and to reinstate themselves as the center of their own lives. The truth is that women actually blossom, rather than fade, at midlife.

Studies done by Ravenna Helson and Geraldine Moane of eighty-one women, initially when they were college graduates, next as young adults, and again in their early forties, discovered that in midlife traditional femininity decreased as confidence increased. Women in their early forties said they were "being my own person; feeling more confident; having a wider perspective; focusing on reality and meeting the needs of the day without being too emotional about them; having influence in my community or area of interest; feeling secure and committed; feeling a new level of productivity and effectiveness; feeling powerful; and having interests in things beyond my own family."

Why We Give Birth to Ourselves at Midlife

There are three essential factors that allow a woman to experience a sense of renewal and rebirth at midlife.

The first involves one of the central tasks of midlife—accepting one's mortality. As we realize that time is finite—we have an expiration date; this isn't a dress rehearsal—women often get more protective of their time. We begin to set clearer boundaries for ourselves, saying no more often. We are less interested in obligatory or unfulfilling relationships. We're more willing to say what we want and need, even when it inconveniences someone else. We're more likely to ask for support rather than assume unnecessary responsibility. If we're going to embody who we truly are, we must start now.

While puberty signals a girl's entrance into the sexual mainstream, menopause is the doorway that allows a woman to step free from our culture's definition of women as sex objects and childbearers. In many respects, menopause is the opposite of puberty. Just as women are coming into their own, they become invisible in our youth-worshiping culture. I know it's upsetting, especially since most of us still feel attractive. (This is when you wish you were living in Europe, where older women are still appreciated.) But while this lack of visibility can be difficult, it also brings good news. It allows us to redefine ourselves and our sexuality, not in terms of "youthfulness," but in terms of self-confidence, acceptance, and expressiveness.

As we shift away from the stereotypes of beauty, we discover the power to define ourselves in our own terms. Women realize that losing their youthful looks doesn't mean losing power—quite the opposite. Their lives can be richer and fuller than ever. As we're no longer bound by society's constricting influences, we can become more self-directed. A new vitality emerges, what pioneering anthropologist Margaret Mead called "pmz"—post-menopausal zest. We discover the freedom to write our lives based on our own vision for our future.

Our past, though, is essential to our future. And midlife, as novelist Joyce Carol Oates puts it, is a "looking back time." There's a direct connection between where we've been and where we're going. From the vantage point of midlife, we gain perspective on the successes we've achieved, the dreams we abandoned, and the themes that have run through our lives. With this new understanding comes an increased ability to focus on who we are and what we need.

One of the consistent themes that emerged from my talks with women was that of a greater sense of acceptance, based on an openness to all aspects of themselves. As we're able to take stock of the totality of our lives and to embrace all of our experiences, even those we would rather forget, we discover a more genuine life. Everything we have done, everyone we've loved, every mistake we've made, every obstacle overcome—all are part of the woman we are today.

Midlife is a time when we are aware of the many compromises we've made. If you chose to stay at home with your children, you may regret that you didn't try your competence in the larger world. If you worked, you may regret that you didn't spend more time with your kids. This awareness of where we have been and the choices we've made is the first step in implementing change.

The Journey Home

At midlife, women experience a longing for a connection with "something" that they can't quite describe but which they know they've been missing. "We forget all too soon the things we thought we could never forget," essayist and novelist Joan Didion writes. "We forget what we whispered and what we dreamed. We forget who we were." There's a hunger to go deeper in our lives, to move beyond the outer trappings of the world, to connect with something larger—to return home.

Midlife is a rite of passage in which a woman will shift her focus inward and recommit herself to deeply held values and beliefs; a rite in which she will find her own voice and rediscover her strengths; a rite in which she can recognize a more authentic self beyond her roles as mother, wife, caretaker, career woman, daughter.

The only thing we can truly claim is ourselves. Not the self we constructed to ensure our survival as children, nor the facade we adopted to be socially acceptable. Not the woman who abandoned her dreams and made others the center of her life. Nor the woman who was continually trying to prove herself. Now is the time to step free of our false self. The effort to sustain it is both draining and self-defeating, and it requires too much energy to maintain.

At midlife, we feel a sense of relief that comes as we begin to peel away everything that's not essential, and discover a truer identity. This means risking other people's disapproval, expressing our thoughts and feelings, even those that are not socially acceptable. Midlife is a psychological search and rescue mission. We must comb back through our lives and recover our spontaneity, outspokenness, enthusiasm, self-confidence, knowledge—the threads of our true selves we lost along the way. We must weave them back into the tapestry of the woman who is emerging. If women can begin to accept the physical, psychological, and spiritual changes that occur during midlife as a natural phase in their development, then they can embark on this journey not with fear but with anticipation. They can experience midlife as a time of immense opportunity—as a time of growth and transformation, as a time to be celebrated.

By the sheer magnitude of our numbers—36 million women had reached midlife by 1999, and the numbers will increase by another 5 million by 2005—we are inventing a New Middle Age. Women of the baby-boom generation are going to change the notion that at middle age women become invisible, sexless, and powerless now that they're no longer pictures of youth. We're going to reverse the belief that midlife is a dead end, a time of loss and decline. The opposite is true. Midlife is a time of rebirth. No, we're not going to change popular opinion overnight. But we are going to change it. As we embrace this rite of passage, not only will we shape the second half of our own lives but we'll set an example for the generations of women to come.

Chapter 2

STRUT YOUR STUFF EVEN IF IT'S SAGGING

The day I buried my youth I grew twenty years younger.

—GEORGE SAND

I never imagined myself becoming a middle-aged woman. Middle-aged women were other women—older, proper, grown-up women. They had wrinkles, age spots, sagging breasts, cottage-cheese thighs. When I looked at my mother, my aunts, my friends' mothers, I always thought of them as "the other," women of another time, another species—the "not me." I knew I was never going to look like them.

While I still felt like a girl inside, there was no denying the reflection I saw in the mirror, especially the full-length mirror. Everything was heading for the floor. But when I looked at myself, it was still me, although it was a different me than I was used to seeing. One day, as I was sitting at the kitchen table sewing a button on a skirt, I looked down, to see my mother's hands, minus the chipped red nail polish. Still, for a time, I denied that I'd changed, until the final blow came.

My twenty-six-year-old daughter was home for a visit. I was getting ready for bed when she walked into the bedroom, looked at me, and said, "Mom, do you think I'm going to get raisins and have yams when I get older?" She was referring to the age spots that were blanketing my body and my sagging breasts. That was it. I remembered the horror I felt when I watched my mother wriggle into her girdle or I saw her flesh oozing from the tight elastic around her legs as she strutted down the beach in a bathing suit, and I knew exactly what my daughter was thinking and feeling. There was no denying it: I had joined the ranks of a group I never thought I would belong to. It was quite a shock.

Every day as we're greeted by the stranger in the mirror, we're reminded that we're no longer the girl we once were. In her place, a woman we barely recognize has appeared. We wonder what's happened to us. And it takes some time to figure out.

If you're still in denial about having reached middle age, the arrival of your invitation to join AARP and your first copy of *Modern Maturity* will certainly force you to face this sobering fact. How do they find us? They're the age police. They have a database like the IRS. They're watching us. They're worse than Big Brother and they're going to blow our cover. I think that even if you joined the witness protection program, they'd still find you. There's no place to hide. Our time has come, and everyone's going to know it.

For those of you who haven't yet hit the big 5-0, let me offer you a warning. Several months prior to your fiftieth birthday, the dreaded envelope will arrive in your mail, inviting you to become a member of AARP—okay, if you're too young to know what the letters stand for, it's the American Association of Retired Persons! I know. None of us is anywhere close to retirement age and we never will be. Nonetheless . . . In my case, I didn't have the option of immediately burying the envelope in the garbage. A so-called friend bought me a membership as a fiftieth birthday present. How depressing. The people at AARP don't realize that we feel that we're way too hip to want to join their organization. I don't care if there are lots of perks, hell no . . .

But I have a confession. Last week, while I was sitting in a doctor's waiting room, I noticed a copy of *Modern Maturity* that had an interview with Gloria Steinem. I made sure that no one was looking as I quickly folded the cover back. I hate to admit it, but not only did I thoroughly enjoy the article but I found it informative. No, I didn't subscribe. That would still have been too big a step for me. But there was a crack in my armor. Ladies: there's no denying it—we're getting older. Okay, say the word. We're middle-aged.

I don't know about you, but have you noticed that we boomer women look pretty darn good? While we're certainly healthier, sexier, and younger-looking than women our age in preceding generations, we're still confronted with the stigma of aging. It wasn't long ago that middle age was considered the beginning of the end for women. The label of "older," at least for women, meant worthless, sexless, invisible, over-the-hill. It was assumed that we would suddenly mutate into frumpy old women wearing muumuus and false eyelashes and sporting bad dye jobs. Midlife was seen as a wasteland, a time filled with loss— the loss of femininity, power, beauty, and youth.

With the onset of midlife, women are caught in a double bind: Despite the inevitable changes in our bodies, we're expected to continue to look young. But as Germaine Greer observed in *The Change,* "A grown woman should not have to masquerade as a girl in order to remain in the land of the living." The more a woman has depended on her appearance for her self-worth, the more vulnerable and insecure she is likely to feel as her youth and beauty fade.

We no longer pretend that we can trade on our looks the way we did when we were younger. Those days are gone. It's time to find something deeper—more enduring—to count on. Our bodies and appearances are in a continual state of change. But our authentic selves remain constant, undiminished by time. This is a revolutionary idea, one that goes against the dominant culture. We forget that we no longer have to go along with the game. We're grown women. And by the sheer magnitude of our numbers, we can invent a New Middle Age. Consequently, we can redefine the rules for aging and attractiveness.

Who Stole the Spotlight?

Our generation invests more energy, time, and money than any other generation in an attempt to stave off the hands of time. In 1997, we spent $1.3 billion on antiaging products, and that's expected to triple by 2002. We've always been trendsetters, in part because there are so many of us. As the children of the fifties and sixties, we helped to shape society's obsession with youth and beauty. We enthroned Twiggy, the stick-thin, innocent adolescent as the symbol of feminine beauty. But now we no longer see ourselves reflected in society's image of the ideal woman. Pick up any magazine; the model on the cover doesn't look like us. Even the ads on television for wrinkle cream use younger models. Our looks are no longer the gauge for beauty. Rather, we're bound by an impossible norm, which subscribes to a "one size fits all" form of beauty—adolescent beauty.

The irony is that just as we're coming into our own, we suddenly become invisible. Our aging bodies seem to betray us. They hinder our reaping the rewards of all that we've worked for and achieved. The message midlife women received is that it's all right to mature, as long as you continue to look young. How do we pull that one off without a visit to the plastic surgeon?

Despite our accomplishments in careers, motherhood, and relationships, many women are often still plagued by the fear that if they don't look the way they're supposed to, their self-worth is threatened. The realization of how much we've depended on our physical appearance is often an uncomfortable awakening. I don't know about you, but even on my best days, I'm not turning heads when I walk down the street. And instead of receiving looks of lust or longing, we more likely have to settle for looks of respect and courtesy. Let's face it, no matter how good we may look or feel, we're simply no longer in the gene pool. But as Betty Friedan points out, "The attempt to hold on to, or judge oneself by, youthful parameters blinds us to the new strengths and possibilities emerging in ourselves." As we step out of the spotlight, we often have mixed feelings. For many women, this may be the first time in their lives that they're not getting the attention they're used to. And while there is a sense of loss in giving up our youth and the ability to command male attention, there's also a freedom that comes from unchaining ourselves from the bonds of appearance. Still, it is an adjustment. A woman may feel disoriented and worried when she first begins to disengage from the power of others' judgment.

The Cult of Youth

None of us forgets adolescence. Our appearance took on such significance—to be chosen, accepted, approved of, or to be left out, alone, unpopular. In adolescence, girls become objects evaluated as either desirable or not based on their looks. As I mentioned in the previous chapter, Harvard professor Carol Gilligan has observed that prepubescent girls were outspoken, bright, enthusiastic, but a radical shift occurred when they became teenagers: They became self-conscious, preoccupied with their image, and their focus changed to catering to and attracting boys.

"When I started junior high, I spent hours poring over *Seventeen*. It was my bible," Natalie, a forty-eight-year-old architect, said to me. "I set my hair on huge brush rollers; I did bust-building exercises, and sit-ups to flatten my stomach. School was all about checking out the 'in crowd,' to see what the prettiest girls were wearing or how they did their hair. When I got home, I would lock myself in the bathroom to see if I could make myself look more like them."

When girls stare in the mirror, they're measuring them-selves against an impossible standard of beauty, and this continues to be true for us today. Teenage girls are so con-cerned with how they're supposed to look that they can no longer see themselves clearly. Rather than thinking about how they feel about themselves, girls become overly con-cerned with how they're going to appear to others. This ex-ternal focus causes a girl to lose touch with herself and her own sense of beauty. What we learned as teenagers doesn't magically disappear over time. Many of us spend the rest of our lives trying to recapture the courage, expressiveness, and self-confidence we had as girls.

Here are a few eye-opening facts about the hoax that has been and continues to be perpetrated on women. Marilyn Monroe wore a size fourteen. If Barbie were a real woman, she would have to walk on all fours because her body is so out of proportion. If shop mannequins were real women, they'd be too thin to menstruate. The average American woman weighs 144 pounds and wears between a size twelve and a size fourteen. One out of every four college-aged women has an eating disorder. The photos of many models in the magazines are airbrushed. A psycho-logical study in 1995 found that three minutes spent look-ing at models in a fashion magazine caused 70 percent of women to feel depressed, guilty, and shameful. Twenty years ago, models weighed 8 percent less than the average woman; today they weigh 23 percent less.

Of the one hundred women I interviewed, as well as the women I see in my private practice, none has ever been completely satisfied with her body. They com-plained about having "thunder thighs," about being too thin, about being flat-chested or large-breasted, about their stomachs pouching out, about carrying ten extra pounds, and the list went on. Women measure their appearance against a fashion god who bestows approval or disapproval based on unrealistic ideals. The image a woman has of herself is often not her own, but, rather, a collage of images that conform to external standards of beauty. It takes years for us to move away from those images. As Gloria Steinem commented in *Revolution from Within*, "It's taken me twenty years to realize I might have asked: Where did that woman in my mind come from?"

Forever Young: The Vanity Crisis

Plastic surgery is on the rise, especially among women. In the United States, 87 percent of all those who have undergone plastic surgery are females. Plastic surgery is the most lucrative specialty in medicine today. The number of liposuction operations increased by 215 percent between 1992 and 1997, according to the latest statistics from the American Academy of Plastic and Reconstructive Surgeons. Plastic surgeons performed 52 percent more face-lifts last year than in 1992; the number of breast enlargements increased even faster.

It isn't that dyed hair or face-lifts are inherently bad. They're not. If a woman feels that her first-edition face or body detracts from her essential self, then why shouldn't she change them so she can feel better? But this is a decision that must be arrived at after self-examination and soul-searching, not out of an unconscious reaction to a fear of aging. We must get beyond the terror of no longer being young.

There are women whose eyelids impair their vision or whose breasts cause them back pain—that's not what I am referring to here. I'm talking about those of us who fervently resist midlife as though it were the end of femininity. Some women invest vast amounts of energy in maintaining youthful looks. Some throw themselves ever more fervently into their careers. Some seek extramarital affairs or new amorous relationships. Many of these women are caught in the crippling fixation of maintaining a youthful image. Only the fates—or a change of thinking—will drag them into their future. There is an old Roman saying: The fates lead those who will. Those who won't, they drag.

If we remain in denial about aging, we rob ourselves of the birth of something important—the rewards of self-knowledge and self-confidence. Cynthia, tall, thin, with shoulder-length blond hair, had recently gotten divorced, after her husband of twenty-three years had left her for a younger woman. Being single for the first time at fifty-one, she felt anxious about her changing appearance. When I went to her office to interview her, she was dressed in a short navy blue skirt, a formfitting woolen v-necked sweater, and high heels. As we talked, Cynthia looked like she wanted to cross her legs but couldn't because her skirt was too tight. "I've been comparing myself with Laura, my husband's new girlfriend," she confided. "I don't have her body or her fresh, young looks. The other day I was at the gym, and I looked at the old ladies in a water aerobics class. Suddenly, it occurred to me that I was one of them. I've always relied on my looks, and now I feel vulnerable and old.

"My husband used to tell me how pretty I was. He actually made a big deal about my looks. All of a sudden, I'm alone, and I started looking at myself through my own critical eyes," Cynthia continued, tears running down her cheeks. "The other morning when I looked in the mirror, I noticed that I'm getting cross-hatching on the lines around my eyes. Pretty soon I'm going to be able to play ticktacktoe on my crow's-feet. I decided that was it. I'm going to get my eyes done. I feel like I have to look young in order to be marketable. If you don't have the right packaging, you won't even get looked at."

It was painful to listen to Cynthia. Her fear and desperation were obvious. Throughout her marriage, she had fallen into the trap of relying on her husband to reassure her about her attractiveness. Now she felt lost and insecure. So much of her attention was focused on her appearance and what she needed to do to attract a man. Many women feel as Cynthia does—that they're being pitted against younger women and have to be attractive on younger women's terms.

Cynthia felt that she had too much to lose, that there was too much at stake now that she was back in the dating world. Her rejection of her aging body was a form of self-hatred. She wanted to return to her twenty-year-old self and deny that anything had changed. It's understandable that so many women fear aging. As author Judith Viorst observes, "For if youth is linked to beauty, and beauty is linked to a woman's sexual attractiveness, and her sexual attractiveness is important to her winning and holding a man, then age's assaults on beauty can catapult her into a terror of abandonment."

I Love Me, I Love Me Not: Steadying Our Inner Vision

We women of the baby-boom generation have been trend-setters from birth. We defined "the youth generation." We started "the fitness craze." Now it is time to define aging for ourselves.

Through my own interviews as well as from the research presented in Terri Apter's excellent book *Secret Paths: Women in the New Midlife,* I came to see that redefining our attractiveness is a process. As a woman begins to redefine her own beauty, she often experiences a tentative acceptance of her changing image along with some backsliding. Since so many women have been conditioned from childhood to believe that their appearance is their one and only self, the further they moved away from the ideal of youthful beauty, the more they think that something's wrong with them. Every wrinkle or every age spot is an attack on who we truly are. Consequently, our essential self feels at times like a stranger, someone we'd like to know, but not at the expense of our safety and security. It's no wonder that a woman experiences radical swings between acceptance and dissatisfaction of her appearance. Many of us have tried at different times to stop ourselves from trying to live up to other people's judgments, and now we are finally doing it. But it takes time.

It's Tuesday evening; storm clouds are building in the sky as the women file into one of the meeting rooms at the Children's Museum for our regular women's group meeting. When I bring up the subject of our changing appearances, everyone immediately becomes animated. Each seems anxious to talk about her particular struggle. The women are between the ages of forty-three and fifty-seven; some are married, some recently divorced, and one woman has remained single all her adult life. "I was a hard body. I worked out obsessively, incessantly," began Joanne, a forty-six-year-old woman dressed in loose-fitting white slacks and matching top. "I've always been blessed with a good figure. But if someone had said, 'You have a lot of your identity wrapped up in your package,' I would have denied it. I didn't see it." Until two years ago, Joanne had worked as the CEO of a company she had started. But after ten years, she found that she was not only exhausted but burned-out. She finally recognized how driven she'd been in attaining success, but also in maintaining her youthful self-image. "I didn't want my identity to be connected with how I looked, how glamorous I was, or how much younger I seemed than my age." But despite her realization, Joanne was still on the seesaw, teetering between two distinct attitudes about her appearance. "I still compare myself to how I looked when I was a hard body. But I'm just not willing to do what it takes to stay in that kind of shape anymore."

As Joanne continued, the other women were nodding their heads in agreement. They each expressed a desire to base their relationships on what they now value—being genuine, kind, and truthful. But as Joanne continued, she articulated what several of the other women were also experiencing. "I feel like Sybil—a split personality," she said. "I don't value glamour anymore, but I still wrestle with what to wear and what impression I want to make. I'd like to be over it already, but I haven't reached a place where I can let that go. I still find that sometimes I'll try on six different outfits before I go out to dinner. I get frustrated that I'm still doing that. I know better, but I can't stop, at least not yet. There are more moments of feeling okay about my changing body, but I still have these ghosts that haunt me."

It takes time for a woman to feel her way through the maze of disentanglement. Since adolescence, women have relied on external validation to confirm their sense of attractiveness. Defining beauty in her own terms is a process that evolves as she gains confidence in herself and her own vision.

As the discussion continued, Judy, a forty-three-year-old Realtor and the mother of two, echoed Joanne's struggle. Separated from her second husband for a year and a half, Judy sat curled up on the couch. "I've always gotten a lot of attention for being pretty," she began, as tears welled in her eyes. "But now that's starting to change. I'm deeper than this, really, but I keep thinking about my future, and I feel like I should suck in my stomach and go to a bar. Not really, but there's a part of me that thinks that. I can't suck it in far enough. Now what?"

Throughout her life, Judy relied heavily on her looks. She had been seeing a man for the past few months, whom she didn't want to be with. They had little in common, but she felt stuck when it came to ending the relationship. "I think I've kept him around because he's hungry for my body," she said, "and it was too scary to face being single without feeling desirable." Like several of the women in the group, Judy talked about her struggle to define attractiveness for herself. "I'm embarrassed to admit it, but I'm still stuck on how people see me. I know I let what other people think influence how I feel about myself, rather than being grounded by what I think and who I am. It's changing. Slowly, but it's changing.

"I get glimpses of moving from my center out, but not as often as I would like to," she continued. "It doesn't hold up. It doesn't last through the day. It's like carrying a daisy around without a vase. It just wilts. So by the end of the day, it's gone. But I'm like this starving person in the desert. I am starving for something that has sustainability. I feel like I'm being reoriented to a different way of seeing myself that I think has more staying power. But it's still so elusive."

For Judy, as for many of us, the challenge had more to do with redefining her own sense of attractiveness than it did with simply stepping free of other people's judgments. And like so many of us Judy was torn between longing to feel more secure with an internal sense of beauty and the need for external validation.

In her book *Mirror, Mirror: The Terror of Not Being Young*, Elissa Melamed writes about the struggle that many women face as they confront aging: "I realize that I was obviously dealing with something deeper than some wrinkles and gray hairs. I was feeling divided, divided against myself: a changeless person trapped inside a changing body; a centered person at odds with a needy person; an honest person ashamed of the 'me' who wanted to play the youth game."

The greater a woman's self-confidence, the more other people's opinions diminish in potency. It is only as women experience more of their own sense of power that they can settle into their new self-image. As we begin to rely on an internal image, we recognize that what people are attracted to is our warmth, ease, and our genuine interest in them. It has less to do with physical image and everything to do with our confidence in being fully ourselves.

Redefining Attractiveness

What I learned from the women I interviewed as well as from my regular groups was that women who were further along in midlife had fewer fears about aging. They were more comfortable with the mature self that was emerging. Martha, a paralegal, had never been married. She was dressed in a royal blue batik tunic and matching harem pants. Her long brown hair was pulled away from her round face, which was lined from years of gardening in the intense sun.

"When I look in the mirror, I'm shocked," she said. "Even though I've been heavy all my life, I've always maintained a familiar overweightness, and that's beginning to expand a little. But I don't want to take over the world by just getting bigger. But in spite of the additional weight, wrinkles, and wisps of gray in my hair, I feel much juicier as a woman."

When Martha was younger, she was more insecure and reserved. Now, despite her age and additional weight, she feels a new sense of health, sexuality, and well-being. "I never understood what flirting was. I finally understand it now that I'm fifty-four," she continued. "It's not like I'm running around flirting with a ton of people, but I feel like I'm flirting with everybody, and it's really fun."

For the first time in her life, Martha felt genuinely attractive. When one of the women questioned her about why she thought that was, she replied without hesitation, "I like myself better. Let me back up. I know myself now in a way I never have before. I feel like a picture coming into focus. I'm just more comfortable with myself. It's amazing, but self-confidence is a powerful beauty potion. I think I look better because I feel better."

Martha's measure of attractiveness had been revised as she progressed through midlife. She came to recognize that being attractive is not about perfect features and trendy clothes. "It's about what emanates from the person. I don't think it has much to do with physical appearance really. It's the eyes. It's the brightness. It's the engagement, the continuous involvement with one's world, involvement with people, being alive. It's internal."

Martha was now more aware of her inner richness and uniqueness as a woman. Her increased confidence was allowing her to approach people in a way that was not possible when she was younger. She had discovered a new sense of attractiveness. It was about maximizing her physical appearance and connecting with her intrinsic sense of worth. Martha had become more connected with her authentic self, and that had allowed her to feel more vital and sexy.

In a 1973 interview in *Harper's Magazine*, novelist Doris Lessing said, "You only begin to discover the difference between what you really are, your real self, and your appearance, when you get a bit older. . . . A whole dimension of life suddenly slides away and you realize that what in fact you've been using to get attention has been what you look like. . . . It's a biological thing. It's totally and absolutely impersonal. It really is a most salutatory and fascinating thing to go through, shedding it all."

The girl we once were is gone. She's been replaced by a more mature self, but one that isn't as readily embraced by society. Nevertheless, we must accept our changing bodies and devote our time and energy to our emerging self if we're ever going to discover a new sense of attractiveness. In some cases, the experience of redefinition emerges from an increase in a woman's self-confidence and power. "People often mistake me for younger than I actually am," Vivian, a fifty-seven-year-old employee recruiter, said with a laugh. "Of course, Clairol helps, but the fact that I don't have any wrinkles, I think, makes a big difference. But I think that beyond being well preserved, my sense of attractiveness comes from feeling more confident and that there's a place for me in the world. When I was a kid, black wasn't beautiful. I was one of a handful of black kids in a predominantly white school. There was no way I was going to be thought of as pretty. So I went through most of my life being a harsh critic of my appearance. There were no black models back then, no beauty products specifically for us. Talk about feeling invisible.

"I can remember when I was in my twenties," Vivian continued, "a friend and I went into Orbachs department store and the saleswoman followed us around like we were going to steal something. What an insult. We felt so intimidated that we never bought the makeup we went for. We just left. That doesn't happen anymore. When I was twenty-five, my career choices were pretty slim. I started in the mailroom, and I've worked myself up to VP of recruitment. I have to admit, I feel like pretty hot stuff. Yeah, I look good, but that, combined with how I feel, is unstoppable. Despite what anyone says, being fifty-seven is pretty great. I feel like I get better every year." The combination of a changing social climate, life experience, and self-confidence afforded Vivian a sense of freedom that she never could have imagined earlier in her life.

Not one woman I talked with claimed to have sailed through the shock of meeting "the stranger in the mirror."

But with that shock comes a freedom many of us have not experienced since we started to menstruate. We're returning to a time in our lives when we were less self-conscious and placed far less attention on our looks. Now that we no longer fit within the realm of ideal beauty, we step out of the spotlight. In doing so, we can enter a period in which we're restored to the passionate, enthusiastic, vital young woman who existed before menstruation. Carolyn Heilbrun writes, "Once past 50 if they can avoid the temptation of the eternal youth purveyors, the sellers of unnatural thinness and cosmetic surgery, they may be able to tap into the feisty girls they once were. And if, at adolescence, the importance of their own convictions had been reinforced, they might at 50 be ready to take on risk, display a newfound vitality and bid good-bye to conventional limitations."

As author Terri Apter notes, during midlife a woman rediscovers "an interest in her body as something that is her own, whose meaning she constructs." She begins to think about what's healthy, what brings her pleasure, what physical expressions are appropriate. Women now become fully conscious caretakers of their own bodies. As they take back their power, there's a new investment in their body as a sacred vehicle for their self-expression.

Banishing Your Inner Critic

There are more and more role models for mature beauty, but you have to look for them. These are vital women who not only look terrific but are known for the contributions they make. Think about older women whom you consider beautiful—women like Maya Angelou (1928) and Isabel Allende (1942), who embody sensuality, passion, dignity; Bonnie Raitt (1949), Judith Jamison (1943), and Tina Turner (1939), who emit sexuality from every cell of their beings. Marian Wright Edelman (1939) and Senator Barbara Boxer (1940) are commanding and impassioned; Susan Sarandon (1946), Bette Midler (1945), and Meryl Streep (1949) are smart, magnetic, and talented. Each of these women radiates an inner beauty and authority. Sure, they care about their appearance, but only as one of the many expressions of their essential self. They each are, in their own distinct way, authentic and strong. And, in case you haven't noticed, authenticity and strength are sexy.

If there is one thing that can undermine your self-confidence, it's your inner critic. You know her. She's the one who mentions that your face is starting to look like a road map, how even your earlobes are getting wrinkles. She's the one who shrieks at you about how ridiculous you look as you try on bathing suits. She's the voice of self-loathing. She pummels you the way she did when you were a teenager, scrutinizing every flaw and imperfection. You can tell that your critic is lurking about when you start to feel depressed, discouraged, and don't like yourself very much. She ruins everything.

So what can you do? How do you banish this voice of self-hatred? You send her on an all-expense-paid vacation to the Bahamas, sign her up for the first civilian flight to the moon. But, in all seriousness, you have to fight back. You need to cultivate a nurturing, appreciative voice to counteract her venom. After all, your critic would have you do whatever it took to get you to look like you did when you were twenty. The next time your critic starts in on you, tell her to be quiet. Tell her if she has something to say, she'll have to say it in a nicer way or you don't want to hear it.

In fact, I'd like to recommend an antidote to the injurious self-talk we all engage in. I'd like to suggest that you take a moment and give yourself a message of appreciation for the beautiful, mature, sensual woman that you are. It might sound something like "I love me; I value me." I know it may feel a bit awkward at first, since most of us have been trained to tell other people that we love and value them and it's considered selfish to lavish this kind of attention on ourselves. But it's long overdue. We spend so much time waiting for others, especially men, to acknowledge us. Now we can start to radiate a light from the self-confidence we feel in ourselves. We can reclaim the power to validate our own beauty and worth. Now's the time for us to look beyond the wrinkles and graying hair and to take in our entire image, the image that goes beyond the mirror, beyond the marriage, the children, the career, and encompasses all that we do and who we are.

Perhaps as a part of redefining your attractiveness, you can begin to value what is most essential about yourself. Imagine what difference it might make if you regularly gave yourself this message of appreciation: "I love me; I value me." As you increase your self-esteem, by nurturing and loving yourself, you begin to break down the self-destructive internal dialogue and discover greater self-acceptance.

If you need some inspiration, here's a story that should provide some. There was an article in the *New York Times* about a group of English women from the Rylstone Women's Institute. Every year, they produce a calendar filled with images of watery sunsets and hiking paths. However, this year, when one of the women's husbands died of cancer, they decided to use the calendar as a fund-raiser for cancer research. To boost their sales, they substituted pictures of themselves wearing only a strand of pearls—that's right, they posed in the buff. The women range in age from forty-five to sixty-six. Much to their surprise, the calendar sold out. The demand was so overwhelming that they've now gone back for a second printing. The calendar is now available in the United States.

Getting Some Perspective

"I'm kind of amazed when I hear my women friends complain about getting wrinkles and gray hair. I want to scream, I hope I live long enough to be able to experience these things," a fifty-one-year-old cancer survivor told me. Few women appreciate how fortunate they are to have their health until they either have a brush with death or experience an illness. Suddenly, they realize how much they rely on their body. Even if you have been spared illness or the loss of a loved one, it's essential that you reconsider the place appearance plays in your life: In the larger scheme of things, it's relatively insignificant.

Perhaps it's time to cultivate an attitude of appreciation and gratitude for how well your body has served you, for your health and all that you have. When you go for a walk, give thanks for the legs that carry you, for the body that so perfectly houses your spirit and makes life possible. When you look into the face of someone you love, say a silent thank-you. When you walk through your front door, be grateful for your home, your pets, and the comfort they provide. When you look in the mirror, be thankful for the years you have lived and the experiences that are still to come. Your wrinkles are badges of distinction. You've earned them. They're a reminder of the life you have lived and the experiences that have made you who you are today. Get into the habit of saying thank you for the little things in life, the unrecognized blessings. Gratitude makes us aware of the richness of life. It's an act of remembrance.

More Than Just a Pretty Face

It isn't that middle-aged women no longer care how they look; they do. Think about the last time someone told you you looked good. Admit it—you lit up. We all do. Appearance is still important, but there has to be something in between letting yourself go and being overly concerned with your looks.

Each woman has to discover what's right for her, what makes her feel attractive. Then she needs to spend enough time so that she's comfortable, confident, and relaxed with her appearance. My friend Valerie wouldn't think of starting her day before her morning ritual. She blow-dries her hair, puts on some eyeliner, a tinted sunscreen, lipstick, and concealer. She does it for herself because it makes her feel good. As she says, "I just give mother nature a hand."

Most of us have spent years asking ourselves, "How do I look?" and then waiting for that magical voice to tell us that we're the fairest in the land. The next time you look in the mirror ask, "How do I feel?" I know it might seem a bit strange, but how you feel about yourself affects your appearance more than how well you're put together.

If you recall the times in your life when you felt the most attractive, you'll discover that they were about more than just your physical appearance. When I think of the times in my own life when I've felt the most beautiful, they were: on my wedding day; when I gave birth to my daughter; at her graduations from high school and college; the day I received my master's degree; the day we surprised my mother with a seventy-fifth birthday party; when I crossed the finish line after having ridden my bike fifty miles. Love, passion, joy, and self-confidence are powerful beauty potions. What they say is, I know who I am, I like who I am, and I'm going to celebrate it regardless of what Madison Avenue or anyone else thinks.

The fashion industry is more concerned with conformity than with individuality. But your appearance is an expression of your uniqueness. The poet e. e. cummings said, "To be nobody but yourself in a world which is doing its best, night and day, to make you everybody else means to fight the hardest battle which any human being can fight, and never stop fighting." Become discerning about the pressures of advertisers and the media and intervene before their messages make you feel unattractive and inadequate. Remember, they want to sell beauty products, so they have a vested interest in keeping you insecure.

Finding Your Own Style

Women change their look throughout their lives. As their inner sense of themselves changes so, too, does their wardrobe. Your style should reflect the woman you are within. Your style emerges from knowing who you are and using your clothes as an extension of your self-expression. Midlife, when so much about you is changing, is a perfect time to experiment and discover a style that works for you now. Go through your closet; try things on. Keep only those things that feel like you and that you look beautiful in. As you clear out your past fashion incarnations, you make room for clothes that will reflect the woman you are becoming.

Nurture your personal style. Invite a girlfriend to go out to your favorite stores and play dress-up. Try on things you wouldn't have considered wearing before. Experiment. You'll discover that different clothes bring out different aspects of your personality. Buy and wear only clothes that you love and that mirror your inner essence..

After the last lecture I gave, I ended up with two raging blisters on my feet. I decided I was no longer going to suffer for the sake of beauty. I didn't care how flattering heels were; I wasn't going to wear traps on my feet any longer. Limping wasn't my idea of fun. When I returned home, I went on a rampage. I was determined that I could look beautiful and be comfortable at the same time.

I rooted through my shoe collection and pulled out my once beloved Charles Jourdan and Ferragamo heels. Then I hit my closet. Out went anything with a tight waistband or that was made of itchy material or was uncomfortable in any way. Next, I purged my underwear drawer of all of my underwire bras. They were pretty and certainly lifted my sagging breasts, but they left horseshoe-shaped marks on my chest. I took it all to the Hospice Thrift Store.

I have to admit that this required a leap of faith. I had

felt secure in my old tailored image, but it no longer felt like me. My cleaning frenzy left a gaping hole in my wardrobe. But it gave me an opportunity to buy things that more closely reflected how I felt about myself now.

I've always felt a bit unsure of myself when it comes to shopping. But to my amazement, I had a much clearer sense of what I liked and what looked good. I discovered casual, unstructured rayon skirts, pants, and tops in complementary colors that I could mix and match. I found flats, boots, and wedgies that were stylish while being comfortable. Pretty quickly, my new look evolved. I was pleased to discover that comfort did not exclude sensuality and sexuality. It simply freed me from living in fashion hell.

Living Longer, Living Better: Rediscovering Your Body

Baby boomers are healthier, fitter, and live longer than any preceding generation. In 1900, the average woman lived to be only 47.3 years. By 1989, her life expectancy had increased to 75.3 years. What's more, the prognosis for older people is even more positive. If you live to be sixty-five, research predicts that you can expect to live another 18.8 years, or until eighty-four.

But your longevity is, to a great extent, dependent on how well you care for your body. At midlife, it's essential that you develop a new relationship with your body. This means learning to appreciate the beauty of functionality. Your body is the vehicle through which you express yourself and your life. When something's wrong with your body, when you're in pain or feeling out of sorts, you can bet that everything else in your life is affected. For those women who have ignored their body, midlife is the time to rediscover it.

At midlife, exercise becomes even more important. We lose muscle tissue as we age. While some of this loss is due to normal aging, more is attributed to inactivity. Studies show that women who remain active throughout midlife have similar muscle tissue, metabolic rates, and only a minimal weight gain when compared to younger women.

A woman's bone density begins to decline well before midlife, but bone loss increases dramatically after menopause. While all forms of exercise are somewhat helpful to protect your bones, weight-bearing activities such as walking, jogging, and cross-country skiing, are the most beneficial. Along with these kinds of activities, you should include some form of weight training that'll help you to maintain muscle tone and overall strength. The increase in muscle strength that you gain from weight training is especially beneficial to women, who are often weak in their upper bodies.

If possible, try to do twenty minutes of aerobic activity at least four days a week and strength training at least twice a week. If you're a confirmed couch potato, it's not too late to change. In a Harvard study, women who went from doing little or no exercise to moderate exercise had a fifty percent decline in the rate of death from all causes. A regular exercise regimen will also help to prevent or delay high blood pressure, heart disease, and other chronic health conditions associated with aging.

While we're barraged with an ever-changing list of fitness programs, it's important to find a form of exercise that you enjoy and will stick to. It may be a combination of walking and weight training, or jogging, swimming, biking, or a samba class. Do what you can do on a consistent basis. But do something. Not only will it improve your health but you'll feel better and look better, too.

Jean, a fifty-one-year-old salesclerk and mother of three, had a rude awakening. "I'm used to going regularly to aerobics, but this was a break-dancing class, which I hadn't been to before," she confessed. "It was at the local college, so it was me and all these college students. I was about halfway through when the instructor said, 'Now we're going to stand on our hands.' I thought to myself, No problem. I used to do that. He divided us into pairs. Here I was with this twenty-something hunk standing next to me, smiling in encouragement. I thought, What the hell. I took a deep breath, went up on my hands, and my arms gave way and I landed on my head. I didn't really hurt myself, except maybe my pride. But it was at that moment that I knew that those days were over. As I sat on the side of the room and watched the other people, I felt a twinge of sadness. I had this conversation with myself about how I used to be able to do that without thinking about it, and I just couldn't do that now. It was a moment when I felt like I'd turned a corner. I hung out in the class for a few more minutes and then I left before the end. It really shook me up."

Jean had realized that something was different. Her body was changing, and she could no longer push it the way she had earlier in her life. Jean continued to do aerobics, but she wanted to do something that would challenge her in a new way.

"A friend had recently taken up spinning," she continued. "You know those specially designed bikes that you ride till you're ready to drop? I went to a class with her, and the teacher was this enthusiastic Australian woman. Boy, did she work us. I went through two towels. I couldn't do everything, but I did most of it, and I finished the class. It was great. I got such an amazing workout. I was stoked that I could keep up."

No, most of us can no longer do break dancing. But there are plenty of other physical challenges we can find to keep ourselves feeling fit and strong. I know women in their fifties who've taken up boxing, tae kwan do, downhill skiing, or ballet for the first time. My friend Celeste ran a ten-kilometer race for the first time at fifty-two and placed third in her age group. Another woman I know climbed one of the fourteen-thousand-foot peaks in Colorado when she was fifty-five. Yet another woman was inspired by her nine-year-old son to take up surfing at the age of fifty-one. All of these women want to feel vital and fit. It's less about having a hard body and more about staying strong and in shape. Your body is a wise teacher. Listen to it. Become attuned to its changing needs.

Along with regular exercise, it's essential that you recommit yourself to a healthy diet, stress reduction, and cutting your excesses. This doesn't mean you can never have another piece of Godiva chocolate, buttered popcorn, or a margarita. Just don't overdo it. We simply don't have the tolerance we used to. When we overindulge ourselves, it's usually a sign that we're neglecting to nurture ourselves in more positive ways.

There's a strong connection between how you feel about your body and your self-esteem. To the extent that you love and appreciate yourself, you're more likely to nurture yourself. But regardless of how well you've taken care of yourself in the past, you can take small steps toward better self-care.

If you don't already pamper yourself, start immediately. I know, some of you may think it's self-indulgent, but, contrary to what we've been taught, there's nothing wrong with being selfish from time to time. In fact, there's everything right with it. Give yourself permission to imagine what you'd consider pampering. Get a massage, take a candlelit bubble bath, buy scented body lotion, play soothing music, schedule a facial, or take a walk alone in the woods. Do something that sends a message to your body that you honor and appreciate how well it serves you.

Beauty standards are in a constant state of flux. Victorian women wore bustles to pad their derrieres. Fashion in the 1920s dictated that busty women wear chest-flattening bras. Then, in the 1940s and 1950s, brassieres that emphasized a woman's bosom were the rage, as well as girdles to hide their hips. From one season to the next, the image of perfect beauty is impossible to keep up with. Dare to reject society's ideal of attractiveness and decide for yourself what is beautiful within you. It will inevitably be as individual as your thumbprint.

Chapter 3

THE *M* WORD

I want to live to be an outrageous old woman
who is never accused of being an old lady.
I want to live to have ten-thousand lovers in one love.
One 70-year-long-loving-love.
There are at least two of me
I want to get leaner and meaner sharper edged
color of the ground till I discorporate
from sheer joy.

AUTHOR UNKNOWN

I know, on some level you thought, It's not going to happen to me. Most of us do. No matter how much we've heard about menopause or know that it's going to happen, the reality comes as a shock. As with childbirth, there's nothing anyone can say to you to prepare you for this mysterious and elemental change. But, unlike having a baby, everyone must experience this. Menopause is an equal-opportunity transition. No one is exempt. Everyone goes through it—the woman who sells you stamps at the post office, the attorney general of the United States, the CEO of Hewlett-Packard, mothers, single women, minority women, lesbians, straight women. Yes, despite all "the work" she's had done to keep herself looking eternally young, it even happens to women like Cher. Menopause is the great equalizer. While we all go through it, there's no "one size fits all" menopause. Our experience is as unique as our DNA.

Shrouded in embarrassment, fear, and confusion, menopause has gotten a bad rap in our culture. I'm not going to pretend that hot flashes, mood swings, and night sweats aren't enough to make a girl want to vacate her body and return when this little inconvenience is over. But since the turn of the century, menopause has been treated like a disease rather than as a healthy, natural, inevitable, biological change.

Women's bodies during menopause are commonly described in medical texts in terms of "functional failure," since they're no longer involved in childbearing. This attitude assumes that a woman's value is tied to her ability to bear children. While this view is still pervasive in much of the world, liberated women know better. In our culture, however, women are thought to lose their femininity when they go through menopause. I think the French feminist Françoise Giroud said it quite well: "As though femininity is something you can lose the way you lose your pocketbook: hmm, where in the world did I put my femininity?"

The personhood of a woman hardly ends with menstruation. Quite the opposite. This biological transition gives us a chance to reconstruct our identities as people whose value and self-esteem extend well beyond our sexuality and motherhood.

In societies where older women gain power and freedom and are revered as they age—in China, Japan, Malaysia, Indonesia, for example—there are fewer, if any, psychological and physical symptoms. Whereas in the United States, where women are valued for youthfulness, they often have a much more adverse reaction. Given our cultural attitude, it's not surprising that for many women menopause is mistakenly thought of as the beginning of the end.

Menopause is one of the most misunderstood transitions in a woman's development. Despite the negative connotations associated with it, menopause is a doorway to a new stage in a woman's development. It is truly a "change of life," rich with opportunities for deeper self-awareness and growth.

The Second Puberty

Menopause has become one of the major health topics of our time. With 50 million women currently experiencing menopause and the explosion in the menopausal population of the United States that will occur over the next two decades, menopause has definitely come out of the closet. Now it's time to change society's attitude about menopause and to normalize this natural physical process. Women need to talk more about menopause. We need to share our experiences so that no one is left feeling like the Lone Hot Flasher.

Remember all the gossip about who'd gotten their periods and what to expect? It took several years to become familiar with the dramatic changes in our bodies when we began to menstruate. I don't know about you, but for quite some time, I felt like I'd been snatched by aliens. My body felt strangely unfamiliar. I was unsure of who this moody, sex-crazed girl was as she was tossed around by raging hormones. Well, here we are again. Menopause is a second puberty. Only now we have to get used to not getting "our friend." And it's going to take several years for us to adjust once again to this hormonal shift. The average woman completes the transformation of perimenopause and emerges into the postmenopausal years when she is 48.4 years of age.

While there are many challenges associated with this change, it is a time of tremendous freedom. Remember all those times you sweated bullets because "your friend" was late? Well, those days are over. This is true liberation, sexual and otherwise. Unlike our mothers, we are not the silent generation. We're going to talk about menopause, complain about it, educate ourselves on how best to care for ourselves as our bodies change, and begin to shatter the stigma associated with this phase of a woman's life.

The Great Hormone Debate: What's a Woman to Do?

*To take hormones, or not to take hormones: that is the
   question:
Whether 'tis nobler to suffer
The slings and arrows of outrageous hot flashes,
Or to take drugs against a sea of tumultuous symptoms,*

*And by taming them to sleep—perchance to find relief
and sanity once more.*

There's no simple answer to whether you should take
hormone-replacement therapy. While most gynecologists
and internists today think that most postmenopausal
women should take hormones, a woman must decide for
herself. Since the experience of menopause is unique for
each woman, she has to weigh the risks and benefits of
hormone-replacement therapy and choose what will support the needs of her particular body. Because no single
treatment is going to work for everyone.

Contrary to popular medical thinking, menopause is a
natural physiological process, not a disease. By the year
2005, there will be about 50 million women in the United
States over the age of fifty, all of them potential candi-
dates for hormone therapy. And don't think that the medical establishment hasn't noticed. Menopause is big
business. But only 46 percent of postmenopausal women
take or have taken hormone therapy—one of the biggest
reasons that many women reject hormone-replacement
therapy is that they have positive feelings about
menopause. They don't think of it as an illness, so why
treat it? In two separate U.S. studies comparing black
women to white women, researchers found "the African-
American women had a significantly more positive attitude toward menopause" than white women did.

I'm not going to go into the myriad treatments available
to women or the pros and cons of HRT. There are 372 new
medicines being developed to treat menopause. Besides,
the research is continually shifting beneath our feet. In
part, your decision depends on where you fall in terms of

symptoms, your level of discomfort, and family history. Some women find going through menopause reminiscent of the tumultuous emotions they experienced during adolescence. But there are the lucky 20 percent who coast through menopause symptom-free.

Whatever you experience, I recommend that you become an expert on menopause and your changing body and take charge of your health care. Thankfully, we're deluged with an abundance of information. But I would like to recommend several excellent books that offer in-depth information on this ever-changing subject: Gail Sheehy's *The Silent Passage; Dr. Susan Love's Hormone Book;* Dr. Christiane Northrup's *Women's Bodies, Women's Wisdom;* Lonnie Barbach's *The Pause.*

Many Doctors Just Don't Know: Reclaiming Our Authority

Dr. Christiane Northrup notes that from birth, women's normal bodily functions—menstruation, pregnancy, childbirth, menopause—have been thought of as conditions that require medical treatment. As a result, healthy women have had many occasions throughout their lives to come in contact with the medical profession.

For time immemorial, we've allowed physicians a position of unquestioned authority. And in turn, a woman's body is often considered to be under her doctor's control. Many doctors mistakenly believe that women want a cure, when what many of us really want is a better understanding of what is happening to our bodies.

Doctors often lack empathy and understanding when

speaking with their patients, especially about issues re-lated to menopause. Out of the one hundred women I in-terviewed, there were a number who reported feeling "shamed for asking questions" or "made to feel stupid." Why do we have to struggle to feel heard and taken seri-ously when it comes to our bodies? What do women have to do to convince their doctors that they need to feel like active partners in their own health care?

We have to become experts and not rely solely on another person's advice when it comes to our changing bodies. I know you thought you had taken assertiveness training back in the seventies, but here we are again, having to become women warriors tenacious about receiving the kind of med-ical treatment we deserve. If you don't feel that you can talk openly and express your fears and concerns with your cur-rent physician, find someone who's not only knowledgeable but also patient, empathetic, and reassuring. It's essential that you find a doctor with whom you feel there is mutual respect and an openness to discuss any and all of your con-cerns. It does take perseverance and tenacity to find the kind of care that's right for you. But remember, you're es-tablishing an important long-term relationship.

The Betrayal of Our Bodies

"I don't have the stamina I used to have, and it's frustrat-ing," Cathy, a forty-nine-year-old labor negotiator, said to me. "I've always burned the candle at both ends, but I can't push myself the way I used to. I feel like I don't have time for menopause. I know that sounds strange, but it's such a bother. I'd rather go out for popcorn and just skip this part of the movie." For years, Cathy's life was fast-paced and overscheduled. Now that her body couldn't maintain the breakneck speed, she felt irritated that she had to slow down. Many women don't want to be bothered by menopause, but—guess what?—menopause is a fact of life. You don't have a choice about whether you'll go through it, but you can choose how. As we saw from the earlier research on how cultural attitudes affected menopausal symptoms, our attitude does have an impact on how we experience menopause.

Many women have taken their bodies for granted. While we may have given up partying until dawn, we're not accustomed to modifying our level of activity. But no matter how fiercely we may deny that we're getting older, there is no denying that our bodies age. This is most powerfully evident with menopause, when the hormones that have naturally coursed through our bodies for the past thirty-five years gradually decline and then stop. Our bodies experience a shock similar to that when we first started to menstruate. We experience mood swings and physical symptoms, and we often require more rest.

Women often experience increased fatigue when they first begin menopause, as they adjust to the change in their body chemistry. But this changes the further along you are in the process. Margaret Mead talked about how postmenopausal women discover a wellspring of energy and vitality, which she described as pmz, postmenopausal zest. As Gail Sheehy writes in *The Silent Passage*, the biological shift that occurs during menopause is actually advantageous for women. As estrogen and progesterone decline, other hormones increase. A postmenopausal woman has twenty times as much testosterone as she did before she began menopause. This explains at least the physiological basis for the phenomenon of post-menopausal zest and increased assertiveness.

Many women want to carry on as though nothing's changed. They're angry and in denial. They don't want to experience the inconvenience of menopause. But menopause isn't called the change of life for nothing. It's a reminder of how little control we actually have over our bodies, let alone our lives. When we menstruate, our monthly bleeding reminds us that we're linked to cycles and rhythms that connect us to the larger mystery of life. Menopause, too, demands that we question our sense of control.

Last summer, my doctor recommended that I have a bone scan to establish a baseline to monitor bone loss as I went through menopause. When she called me with the results, we were both shocked. I had osteoporosis. I was incredulous. There must be some mistake, I thought. This kind of thing doesn't happen to me. I was sure that the young technician had miscalibrated the machine.

I called the imaging center and asked for a retest. As I lay on the table, tears rolled down my cheeks. I could see from the image on the machine that it matched the other scan. There was no mistake. I walked out to my car and burst into tears. Part of me wanted to pretend that this wasn't happening. It would be easy to do. I couldn't see it or feel it. I looked and felt fine, but I knew better. Denial would only seal my fate of ending up as a frail old woman.

I had been healthy all my life. I go mountain biking, do weight training, hike, and go cross-country skiing. I have a healthy diet. I've never smoked and I don't drink carbonated beverages. I didn't fit the profile, but somehow, unbeknownst to me, termites were gnawing away at my bones, weakening my structure. I began to question many of the things I was used to doing without a second thought. Could I still go cross-country skiing? What if I fell? What about hiking? Would I have to change my lifestyle? I found myself with a case of rampant paranoia. I bought a new pair of hiking boots with a killer tread. I didn't want to fall. Suddenly, the extra padding on my hips was a welcome cushion.

For the first time in my life, I felt as though my body had betrayed me. I felt as though I'd lost the body that had served me so well for all these years. I'd never been sick during my adult life. I had gone to the doctor only for routine exams or, recently, to cope with menopause. I was angry and scared. It wasn't that I had thought of myself as invincible, but I never imagined that I was going to face an illness, never mind this young. Now I was confronted with my own fragility. It just didn't fit my self-image. Suddenly, I had fantasies of turning into a bog woman or ending up as a pile of dust. Not what I had imagined.

Reclaiming the Wisdom of Our Bodies

The osteoporosis forced me to change how I perceived myself and the world. While it was frightening at first, it was another instance of receiving a gift in black wrapping paper—you know, those lessons that come whether we want them or not. I was being asked not only to let go of my image of myself as a young woman but to recognize how much I depended on my body remaining healthy. I began to listen to my body in a way I hadn't before. As

Gloria Steinem put it, "Perhaps one of the rewards of aging is a less forgiving body that transmits its warnings faster—not as betrayal, but as wisdom." Our bodies demand that we shift our focus away from the frenzy of life toward a more mindful way of being. Now a woman can no longer deny the wisdom of her body.

Those of you who bore children might remember how during your pregnancy you were in closer touch with your bodily changes. Regardless of what we may have wanted to do, despite how much we may have wanted to feel that we were running the show, pregnancy taught us the lessons of surrender and attentiveness. We often had to cancel or reschedule plans in the face of our bodies' needs. In a similar way, we must now become attuned to our bodies.

If we treat our menopausal bodies with the same care and amazement that we treated our pregnant bodies, this phase of our lives would be understood for what it truly is—an initiation into the second half of our lives. Perhaps now as we go through this time of immense change, the same nurturing energy that we focused on the new life that was growing within our womb must now be refocused on giving birth to our newly emerging selves.

With menopause, we're compelled to surrender not only to our biology but also to the inevitability of change itself, which can be daunting, if not frightening. Yet learning to accept the continuous process of change, each and every moment, is one of the central lessons offered by menopause. As we experience the change within our bodies, we become aware of our connection with something universal, something eternal. Menopause provides an opening that allows us to touch the sacred, the great mystery of life.

I recently had an experience that helped me to remember how vulnerable we are and the importance of being thankful for my body. I went to my regular Saturday-morning yoga class. After some preliminary poses, the teacher had us kneel facing the wall, with our pelvises touching it. She then instructed us on how to lean back, grab our ankles, and drop our heads into a back bend. I couldn't get near my heels. She noticed me struggling and came around behind me, placed her feet on my back, along my spine, and gently applied pressure as I reached around to grab her arms. Within seconds, I was in tears. She took her feet away and asked if I was all right. I told her that her foot was pushing where I had broken my back twenty-three years ago. She reassured me that back bends often release a lot of emotion. I felt a little embarrassed crying in a class with fifteen other people. I pulled myself together as best I could and did a modified version of the pose.

The instructor then demonstrated the next posture, which was very strenuous. I was certain that I wouldn't be able to do it. After a few failed attempts, the man lying next to me made a suggestion that he thought might help. I made the adjustment and was able to do the pose. I felt such a sense of triumph.

As we lay on the floor in a resting posture at the end of class, tears rolled down my cheeks. I realized how fortunate I am not only to be able to do yoga but to walk, hike, ski—all the things I love but that I take for granted. I felt myself fill with gratitude. I'm not confined to a wheelchair, as doctors once expected. Now, despite the osteoporosis, I feel strong and capable. The feeling of gratitude stayed with me. I was filled with a sense of peace, well-being, and an appreciation for the preciousness of life.

Revisioning Menopause

Menopause is a physiological wake-up call that requires that we pay attention to where we stand in our lives. If the onset of fertility is seen as central to a woman's development, if her ability to conceive is highly valued, how can the conclusion of it not have significance, as well? In many ancient cultures around the world, the passages in a woman's life—the beginning of menstruation, pregnancy, childbirth, menopause—are honored as hallowed rites of passage as well as biological occurrences.

In many traditional societies, the ancient beliefs dictated that shamanic practices be limited to post-menopausal women because it was thought that once a woman stopped menstruating, she retained her "wise blood." In ancient times, there was something called "the blood mysteries." Steeped in the miracle of bringing life into the world, these mysteries involved menarche, the moment at which a girl becomes a woman by menstruating for the first time. Menstruation was an initiatory experience, celebrated and sanctified. People noticed that girls bled once a month, in a way that reflected the cycle of the moon. Only when a woman was making a baby, the thinking went, would she retain the blood within her body for nine months. The cessation of menstruation was acknowledged and celebrated as a time when a woman retained blood in her body, not for the purpose of making a baby but for the purpose of making wisdom.

Among the Maori of New Zealand, the !Kung of Africa, the Druze of the eastern Mediterranean region, as well as in various other cultures, healing powers and esoteric secrets are restricted to members who are middle-aged or older. The postmenopausal woman is revered as wise and powerful. The Kirghiz of Kyrgyzstan believe that you must be at least thirty years old to be a true healer. When a woman stops menstruating, she becomes a priestess, a wise woman.

As Hermann Hesse said in *The Glass Bead Game,* "There is a magic in each new beginning. And if we listen, it will teach us how to live." We must revision menopause. Rather than being viewed as a time of loss, it must be viewed as a time of self-valuing and empowerment. Throughout the process of menopause, we're being asked to discover what is real, true, and enduring about ourselves. Menopause is a soul event, a spiritual passage, which can bring us in contact with our authentic self—the part of us that is eternal.

Birth of the Wise Woman: Please Don't Ask Me to Get Croned!

Someone didn't do their homework when they decided to use the word *crone* as the calling card of the postmenopausal wise woman. According to the *Oxford Dictionary of English Etymology,* the derivation of *crone* comes from *carogne,* meaning "a useless female sheep," or "carrion." A crone is a hag, an old biddy. It's the female equivalent of *geezer.* I don't know about you, but the last thing I want to be is croned, especially since I was just AARP'd.

I know thousands of women are holding croning cere-
monies. No standing naked under the moon, beating
drums, smudging myself with sage, and chanting incanta-
tions for me. When a friend suggested that I have a croning ritual to celebrate my fiftieth birthday, I shuddered.
Instead, my daughter, my friend Georgia, and I went to a
party store and bought Day-Glo feather tiaras. Joined by
four close women friends, we went bowling—in our
tiaras—to celebrate. It was a blast. We were the talk of the
lanes. None of us had bowled since we were teenagers,
and what we lacked in skill, we made up for in chutzpah.
(Don't get me wrong—I've done my share of smudging
and chanting. It's fine to stand naked under the moon and
smudge yourself, but turn yourself into a goddess, a witch,
not a crone!)

But all kidding aside, menopausal wisdom is different
from academic knowledge. It's a wisdom that is rooted in
the truth and experience of our lives: a bone wisdom. This
bone wisdom is only acquired with the passing of time.
The experience of living a full and examined life allows us
to sink deeply into the fertile ground of our being and encounter a unique strength and confidence that was previously unknown.

The founding fathers of the United States modeled the
Constitution on an Iroquois document. But they left out
one tiny detail. In the Iroquois treaty, the women of the
grandmother lodge—the postmenopausal women—had
the final say as to who was to be the chief. They also were
able to say no to any decision that they didn't feel would
support life fully. That was the job of the grandmother
lodge and that is our job today. We must be more willing
to speak our minds and stand up for what we value and be-

lieve in. We desperately need this wisdom now. We must speak out on our own behalf and on behalf of those we love.

Selena, fifty-seven, has been an elementary school teacher for twenty-seven years. Before the end of the school year, the local newspaper reported that the school board could not account for $3 million of its budget. Selena went down to the school board and presented a request for information about the administration. She also filed a formal complaint. She then took copies to the newspaper. "I know I'm going to catch holy hell for this, but, you know what, I just don't care anymore. I'm tired of it. I've spent so much of my life trying to appease everybody and keeping the peace. But I've gotten to a certain point in my life where I don't care if people like me or not. I'm just going to say what I think, and if it gets me in trouble, so be it."

We're no longer so concerned with what people think of us or how much they love us. We're simply going to tell the truth. Have you noticed that women become a little dangerous during this time? We can no longer keep the lid on ourselves. One of the blessings of midlife is that we're no longer willing to silence ourselves. We now feel the necessity to speak.

Humor is another way for us to connect with our wisdom. To be able to laugh at ourselves and to make light even in the midst of a difficult situation is a great blessing. It breaks the intensity. It brings insight and tolerance and allows us to get some perspective. My friend Susan is getting a divorce after twenty-three years of marriage. Understandably, there are times when she goes into a fantasy and loses sight of who her husband is and how miserable she was in the marriage. She called to tell me that while her husband and his new girlfriend, whom he had left her for, had been out shopping to equip the kitchen in their new house, he'd bought her a pair of kitchen tongs and gave them to her when he came to pick up their son. She started to think that maybe he wasn't such a bad guy after all, that maybe he'd changed, and that maybe his new girlfriend was getting what she herself had never been able to get from him. Susan began to embellish the crumbs her husband had thrown her into a luscious cake. I hung up the phone, waited a few minutes, and then called her back. I disguised my voice and said, "Ma'am, this is NASA. I've been asked to deliver the Hubble telescope to your house so that you can see things more clearly." We cracked up. That's become our signal. Anytime either of us starts to lose touch with reality, we say, "get the Hubble." We laugh, but it also reminds us of the truth. It brings insight to a situation in a way that is easier to take. We can say things with humor that we might otherwise not be able to say.

One of the benefits of moving into maturity is that we're more protective of our time and are more willing to say no. We must be willing to say no to some things in order to make room to say yes to others. At midlife, we have the self-knowledge, determination, and experience to make choices in a way we may not have earlier in our lives. Saying no is a way of caring for and honoring one's true self. Now that we have less of a need to prove ourselves or to please others, we can allow the wise woman to speak. When it comes to making a decision, our new criteria should be: "This is the only life I have. Is this how I want to spend my time?" We can ask ourselves this question when someone asks us to go out to dinner, when being offered a new project, when being called on to volunteer for a charity function or in our child's classroom. It's the highest form of self-care, of self-preservation. Being protective of our time and energy is a way to keep in touch with what's most essential in our lives.

This is the time for us to claim all that we've done and all that we are. The wisdom we gain at midlife is paradoxical. The wise woman moves in the world with strength and vulnerability, confidence and humility, and a greater degree of trust in the intangible—her authentic self. As she recognizes just how little she actually knows, she becomes truly wise.

Menopausal Moms

When a woman has children in her late thirties and forties, she is out of sync with the usual development cycle. She can be taking her infant for a well-baby checkup one minute and consulting her doctor about hormone-replacement therapy the next. More and more women are pursuing their careers well into their thirties and postponing motherhood until the last possible minute.

"I had a professional life and got married at thirty-nine. We have an eight-year-old," Linda, a forty-nine-year-old museum curator, told me. "Now I'm swimming in this domestic soup all the time. I'm living two lives simultaneously and I feel uncomfortable a lot of the time. Most women I know got married and had kids when they were young. I did it in reverse. My husband said, 'Don't you want to get married while you're still in your thirties?' So I did. Now I have this part of me that's a middle-aged woman and this other part that's dealing with the issues of younger women. The mother of my daughter's best friend reminded me that I'm her mother's age. That was a real shock."

The memory of being pregnant and nursing her daughter is still fresh, but now that she's about to turn fifty, she's suddenly on the other end of the spectrum. "It just feels compacted. Instead of starting at twenty and having babies like my sister did and then having this solid chunk of time to think about fertility, I crammed it all into a ten-year period," Linda continued. "Last year, I had a garage sale to sell my baby clothes. It felt bizarre to be having a hot flash while selling my breast pump. I have this little kid and I'm taking parenting classes with women who are ten or twenty years younger than I am and then going to a support group for women and menopause. It's just weird."

Women who waited to have children until they were in their forties are often thrust into social situations with women who are far younger and are dealing with a completely different set of life issues. What they have in common is the fact that they have children. But older women often feel lonely and out of place. It's not uncommon for women who have children later in life to feel like they're ricocheting between two intense transitions without enough time to adjust to the change.

Then there are those menopausal moms who are raising teenagers and are dealing with dueling hormones. My friend Celeste is fifty-two and the single mother of a thirteen-year-old son. I asked her what it's like. "If you're in menopause and your kid's in adolescence, that's asking for trouble. My son and I are both suffering from raging hormones," she said. "No one mentioned this when I became a late-in-life first-time mom. And I never thought about it. But there are times when it's hell. I've decided that the only solution is to check him into military school. Or maybe it's me who needs to go. I've never felt so insecure in my life, and I think part of it has to do with my age. I feel crazy and I'm raising an adolescent. Not a good thing. He needs stability and I feel like a Fruit Loop a lot of the time. I think being a single mother makes me feel doubly insecure. There's no buffer, no sane voice to calm things down, and we could certainly use one. Nature has played this cruel joke on me by having us simultaneously hormonally impaired."

There are definite challenges to raising children while going through menopause. Sleep deprivation, fluctuating hormones, and mood swings decrease our tolerance for stress and can make it more difficult to find the elusive patience that's required while raising children. Thankfully, these hormonal meltdowns are temporary. You will regain your sanity and equilibrium before long.

On the positive side, the maturity one has at midlife is an invaluable asset in parenting. Your willingness to make the difficult choices, hold the line when it comes to discipline, and risk your children's disapproval gets easier with age. We simply aren't thrown by the things that would've confounded us when we were younger. So being a menopausal mom is a mixed blessing.

You have to make a concerted effort to take time for yourself, to mother yourself while continuing to nurture your kids. It's essential that you make sure that your needs and dreams aren't buried under the demands of children, husband, and career. No, you don't have the luxury that many women have of fewer parental responsibilities, more time to yourself, the freedom to make love without barricading yourself in your bedroom, but there is something about having children around that keeps you feeling young.

Menopause is a universal experience for women. It binds us one to another in a primal way. During this transition, we have an opportunity to achieve a greater attunement between mind, body, and spirit, between exertion and refueling, vulnerability and strength, control and surrender.

We need to respect and value this passage, rather than ignore it. If we don't, we'll miss an opportunity for transformation. As we learn to surrender to the cycles of our life, we gain a deeper understanding of life itself. Menopause is a time of letting go and of welcoming—a time to notice not only what is being lost but also what can be gained.

Chapter 4

SEX, DRUGS, AND MENOPAUSE

You know the mind is an astonishing, long living, erotic thing.

—GRACE PALEY

As younger women, many of us thought that we were liberated. After all, we were part of the feminist and sexual revolution. But this is the time in our lives when we're truly liberated. Civil rights activist Janet Harris said, "Quite a few women told me, one way or another, that they thought it was sex, not youth, that's wasted on the young." Love does not belong to youth. Now we finally know what's good. We know what we want, when we want it, and we're far more vocal about it. We're less willing to settle for the comfort of a warm body out of fear of rejection or loneliness. And we're finally mature enough to value being appreciated.

During midlife, regardless of whether you're married, single, widowed, or divorced, you have an opportunity once again to explore your sexuality. If you're married, you may have found that your growing children cramped your style when it came to your sex life. With children needing your attention far less or even leaving the nest, it may be time to rediscover your husband and rekindle your passion. For those of us who find ourselves single either through choice, divorce, or the death of a spouse, we have a chance to enjoy our freedom, or seek a new, more equitable romantic relationship with either a man or someone of the same sex. And while sexuality doesn't end with menopause, it frequently does change. Approximately 70 percent of women between the ages of forty-five and fifty-nine are sexually active, and the average frequency of intercourse is one or more times per week.

We're born sexual beings and we continue to be so until we die. No, our present level of sexual appetite and activity isn't going to be what it was when we were in our twenties. But for many of us, the nature of sex has changed. For married women and women in long-term relationships, it isn't simply about passion as much as it is about a deepening intimacy. For divorced, widowed, and single women, it may be more about sexual adventure, romance, exploration of their sexuality, and a newfound sense of freedom.

Midlife sexuality is as unique as a woman's experience of menopause. The myth that the end of fertility is equated with the end of sexuality isn't true. "Because our society views menopause as 'failed productivity' and associates reproductive capacity with sexual capacity, many women have bought the belief that their sex drive is supposed to go away. But in humans, the capacity for sexual pleasure and the capacity for reproduction are two distinct functions. We can always have one without the other."

"At least 50 percent of menopausal women report no decline in sexual interest, and fewer than 20 percent report any significant decline," studies show. "The women's capacity for orgasm is not impaired in any way by aging," Masters and Johnson determined. "In one study, the frequency of orgasm for sexually active women was actually found to increase in each decade of life, through the eighties."

Unexpected Passion

While some women do experience a decline in libido during menopause, others feel a heightened level of desire. For many women, being freed from the fear of pregnancy rejuvenates their sex lives, allowing them to become more sensual than while they were still fertile. A Gallup poll of six thousand people found that 61 percent of married people in their early fifties and 37 percent of those over sixty have sex every week.

"I think there was a birth of sexuality at thirteen, but as I go into menopause, I just feel sexier," Evelyn, a forty-eight-year-old elementary school teacher, explained one evening during our women's group. "God knows, my body isn't especially sexy. I think, What could my husband even see in me? Then I look at his body and I go, Yeah, his is falling, too. But I feel much less self-conscious than I did when I was younger and probably looked a hell of a lot better. I've experienced a change in my sexuality since starting menopause. I feel more comfortable with sex than I've ever felt in my life. We worked very hard to have our children. But as I reach this point in my life where I don't have to worry about having my period anymore, I go, Whoopee. I feel sexier and more aggressive." As Evelyn talked about her relationship with her husband, the support and encouragement she felt from him was obvious. That, combined with fewer responsibilities and her increased sense of comfort with herself and within the relationship, was contributing to the blossoming of her sexuality.

"When you're having kids and everything is so crazy, it's like, Yeah, yeah, it's Friday night, okay," Evelyn continued. "But it's just now that it feels like a rebirth. My husband's home in the mornings and our daughter is gone. There are more opportunities. But it's not just that. It's just different. No, I don't look sexy anymore, but I have a better imagination. Something is changing. I feel good about myself, where I didn't twenty years ago. I'm to the point where I don't turn heads, but I don't care because I don't have to turn his head. I know Tim's there, he knows I'm here, and it doesn't matter if my hips are bigger. I know he loves me."

After years of sharing the same bed, couples know each other better. When a couple has worked through a lot of the emotional issues and power struggles that naturally arise in a long-term relationship, there's often a greater trust and intimacy, and as a result, the sexual bond deepens. Women often discover that men are better, more attentive lovers in midlife. Now that the sexual frenzy of earlier in our lives has diminished, we're able to experience a more relaxed, tender sexual exchange.

For women in long-term relationships, midlife represents a time when they and their partners can enjoy greater intimacy as they experience an increase in self-esteem and self-acceptance. Often, within the safety of a committed relationship, a woman feels freer to be more sexually assertive than she is "supposed" to be. With a foundation of trust, comfort, and confidence, there's room for her to explore what's new within herself and her sexuality.

Many women choose not to remarry after divorce. With increased economic freedom, women are freer to choose the form they want their midlife relationships to take. They no longer feel the need to formalize the union with marriage or even to live with a man full-time.

"My marriage was quite a disaster. As I look back, I don't even know what kind of a sexual being I was then," Alice, a fifty-eight-year-old hospital administrator, said. "I've been in a wonderful relationship with a man for the past thirteen years. I feel accepted and cherished by him. I think I'm lucky to feel as passionate as I do and to enjoy my sexuality as much as I do."

The man lives fifty miles away from Alice, and they only see each other on weekends. Alice relishes living alone and spending time with her lover on the weekends. At one point, they had talked about living together. But when she had to make a decision, Alice realized that she needed her own time during the week. "I'm intensely involved in my work," she said. "And as much as I love my time with Richard, I really like coming home to myself and having time just to respond to what I need. We talk every night. I feel I'm more intimate with him than I've ever been with anybody. So it's not about a continuous presence. I really feel that he's with me."

Alice had been raised in a strict New England Protestant family. "I've probably grown to let myself be more intimate now. I think it's because I'm more trusting and the fact that I feel so completely met," she said. "There's more wildness in my sexuality. My mother made it clear that you weren't supposed to have sex unless you wanted a baby. Never mind pleasure. That was out of the question. So letting myself be wildly sexual has been a real process for me. I love that Richard and I can be playful sexually. We tease and joke, and there's just a sense of freedom and experimentation. It's an unexpected joy." Alice had broken the bonds of her earlier sexual repression and is experiencing a meaningful sexual relationship. While she is deeply committed to the relationship, she has been more actively involved in defining what form it would take to suit her present needs and lifestyle. For many women, especially those who do choose to be in committed relationships, passion now goes well beyond physical chemistry, to include feeling appreciated as a whole person.

Unraging Hormones

Just as some women find an increase in sexual desire during menopause, there are those who experience a decrease in their libido. Among the women I've seen in my private practice as well as those I interviewed, reactions to this change were dramatically different. Some married women who have less sexual interest are not bothered by it, although they are concerned about their husbands. Others choose to see menopause as the end of their sexuality, despite the scientific research to the contrary. If there are unresolved issues in their marriage or they haven't had good sexual relationships in the past, menopause allows women to have an excuse to close the book on sex. Women have found different ways to navigate their change in sexual desire within their marriages.

Patricia and Larry have been married for twenty-five years. They have two daughters, nine and thirteen. Patricia, a fiery redhead with a thick Scottish accent, leads me upstairs to her study, away from the blare of the music videos on MTV. In the course of our conversation, I ask about whether her sexual energy has changed since entering midlife. "Since my periods started to get irregular, I have less drive. So it's not totally surprising that I'm not that interested in sex," Patricia said. "It's actually a relief. Sex has always been an important part of my life. But since having the girls, that's changed. It's changed even more since I've started menopause. Larry and I adore each other and I'm totally affectionate, but I could care less about sex."

Patricia has played a traditional role throughout her married life, putting her husband's needs before her own. For the most part, his sexual desire and appetite dictated their lovemaking. Up until fairly recently, her husband's needs took precedence.

"I'm an old-fashioned woman in many ways. I like to please Larry. I make him breakfast and other meals. I feel like I'm really there for him. But when it comes to sex, it's become a balancing act. There's much more give-and-take between us now than there was when we were younger. Before, I was so concerned with satisfying his needs that I didn't think so much about my own. Not anymore. He's

still interested in lovemaking and it's been a big adjustment for him to realize that if we make love once a week,
that's it. If it were just up to me, I wouldn't bother. I can
take it or leave it at this point in my life. But there are issues at stake here. It's not just me. I don't want to jeopardize our marriage. So I make the effort. I don't think
having teenagers underfoot helps much. Most of the time,
you're too bloody tired anyway. But for me, it's about making the effort, as opposed to being involved in a romantic,
passionate way."

In the past, the frequency of a woman's sexual involvement was often determined more by her partner's sexual
appetite. But as men's sexual needs become less urgent,
women are often more able to respond to their own sexual rhythms, rather than to their husbands' sexual demands. After menopause, a woman's more likely to base
her sexual activity on her level of desire. Not only do
women become more in touch with their feelings but
they're more willing to make them known and to act on
them. Patricia wanted to sustain her marriage, but she
didn't want to ignore her own needs simply to please her
husband.

A Change of Heart

For some women, midlife seems to allow for the possibility of creating a relationship with another woman. Although there's still a stigma attached to homosexuality, at
midlife many women's attitudes toward same-sex relationships seem to ease, allowing for this change in sexual
orientation. At midlife, women are less concerned with

whether people think they're homosexual, bisexual, asexual, or wildly sexual. They're finally more concerned with what will bring them pleasure. Several women I've seen in my private practice have found themselves attracted to women after menopause, despite having always defined themselves as heterosexual.

Dana, a forty-seven-year-old substance-abuse counselor, had been married to an engineer for ten years. Her husband had two grown children from a previous marriage, but they had no children of their own. Dana was unhappy in her relationship. She had come to see me because she was thinking of leaving her marriage. She is a stocky woman with short black hair that frames her moon-shaped face. She wore a pair of loose-fitting rayon slacks and a blousy top covered by a flowered vest. Dana carried herself with a great deal of self-assurance. But as soon as she sat down on the couch, her feelings poured out of her as if the floodgates of a dam had been opened. "I'm married, but I feel completely alone," she began as she dabbed her face with a Kleenex. "Bill and I have slept in separate rooms for the past eight months. He comes in from time to time and makes feeble attempts to talk, but it never goes anywhere. The truth is that he's pretty content with his life. He has his work; he goes flying and hiking with friends on the weekend. He doesn't seem to need or want any more than that. As long as I'm physically present, that seems to be what he considers a relationship. But I'm miserable."

Dana sat quietly for a moment and then looked up at me and said, "I have a secret. I went to a conference on addiction with one of my coworkers a few weeks ago. We shared a room. Rhonda was upset by some of the material that had been presented. When we returned to the room, she asked if I would hold her. We ended up sleeping together. It wasn't sexual. We just curled up together. I've never been held like that in my entire life. The next morning, we talked and talked, and she was genuinely interested in what I had to say. She really listened to me. It was incredible. But I feel out of integrity. I've been spending time with Rhonda and lying about where I've been going. Bill's becoming suspicious. I spent the day with her on Saturday, and then we talked on the phone on Sunday. He wanted to know why I was talking to her after we'd just seen each other."

Over the next several sessions, Dana and I discussed her leaving her marriage. We weighed the pros and cons, and it appeared that there was little to hold her in the relationship. She had asked Bill to go to counseling in the past, and he was adamantly opposed. He thought she was fabricating problems that didn't exist. Consequently, she saw little chance for Bill to change, and she couldn't endure the loneliness. Within a month, she had made up her mind to file for divorce. While Dana was concerned about how Bill would take the news and about her financial situation, she was determined to leave. "I feel like a horse who's been in a pen, with its head hanging over the fence, champing at the bit to get out. I don't think that Rhonda is the love of my life. But at least now I know it's possible for me to get my needs met. That feels wonderful. Bill's not going to understand, but I can't worry about him. I just can't deny myself anymore."

I asked her how she felt about being with a woman. "It really doesn't matter. Man, woman, it's not that important. What's important is that I feel considered. That's all

I care about. Right now, it seems more possible with a woman. I never expected it, but I'm not going to turn down this banquet after I've been starving. I can't."

Women may discover a greater ease in relating to another woman. There's less pressure to maintain a youthful appearance and greater understanding of the physical changes that naturally occur. Women who've chosen to be in a same-sex relationship talk about the fact that they feel their female partners are more loving, considerate, and sympathetic. They frequently experience a level of comfort and ease they hadn't felt with a man. At midlife, women want depth, honesty, equality, and caring, regardless of whom we are involved with.

Sex and the Single Woman

I know that there are some of us who haven't had sex in the past millennium and aren't sure that we ever will again. While some of us are concerned, there are those women who are content with their intentional celibacy. "If you had asked me seven years ago if I ever thought I would go for a long period of time without having sex, I would have looked at you like you were crazy," Kirstin, a forty-two-year-old radio station manager, admitted. "I'm a very sexual person, but I'm just not having sex. I have male friends whom I spend time with. But I'm just not interested in getting sexually involved. I don't think that this is a permanent condition, but for now, I'm perfectly happy channeling that energy in other directions. I've spent a lot of my life in relationships, and now I want to see what it's like to just be on my own."

For some women, the lack of interest in sex comes as a welcome relief. "I just thought sex was a thing of the past," Janet, a tall, dark-haired woman, said. "I had no sexual energy. I didn't even masturbate or have fantasies anymore. Then one Saturday night, I went to a swing-dancing class. I was randomly partnered with a teddy bear of a man. By the end of the night, I felt sparks. I couldn't believe it. It had been so long, I had given up. Now I'm having the best sex of my life, and I'm fifty-two years old. What a surprise."

Yes, sex is different at forty-eight, fifty, fifty-eight, sixty-eight, but no less satisfying. At midlife, when a woman is more financially secure and independent, she often sees sex as a new kind of pleasure, separate from the vulnerability and emotional issues she used to experience as a younger woman. Of course, she may feel insecure about her changing body—but not about who she is and what she wants. At this point in our lives, we're less likely to lose ourselves in another person the way we did at an earlier age. Most of us have a solid grasp of ourselves. We're not going to get swept into another person's life at the expense of our own.

Cecily, a fifty-one-year-old African-American, is an immigration attorney and the mother of two preteen sons. "I really like being this age," she said. "I've become much more sexual since menopause, which is counter to what I would have thought prior to entering it. I've been involved with this man on and off for the past two years. We have this great sexual connection and it's really wonderful. That's been an enormous amount of fun for me. I feel very sexy when I'm with him. From time to time, he brings up spending more time together and taking our relationship to the next level. But truthfully, I don't really want any more than it is."

In the past, Cecily would have thought about their future together. Would he be good marriage material? Would he be a good stepfather to her sons? But she cherishes her independence. "I've done the married thing. Right now, I don't want a full-time commitment. I don't need all the emotional drama that comes with a serious relationship. I have good friends, a close-knit family, and two great kids. So pure and simple, it's great sex, and that suits me just fine."

Women don't always feel the need for commitment and monogamy. Women can now step free of the old stigma of being promiscuous and allow their desire to guide them, but with a maturity and self-assuredness that was absent earlier in their lives.

We're no longer driven by the hormones that propel our passion. Some women turn their attention elsewhere and channel their sexual energy into creative projects, travel, new friendships. Most women, however, tap into a deeper level of their sexuality and feel freer to say, do, and look exactly as they please. We now care more about how we feel than about what other people think. And this shift is tremendously liberating.

Now's the time to make a declaration of independence—to be who it is you truly are. This includes sexually expressing your preferences, needs, aggression, and passion. Only you can throw off the old restraints. You're the one who can bring about your sexual liberation. Isn't it time to be outrageous? What do you have to lose? There's no one left to impress. It's time to please yourself, to be truly, fully, uninhibitedly yourself. The poet Rumi put it well when he said,

Forget safety.
Live where you fear to live.
Destroy your reputation.
Be notorious.

I have tried prudent planning
long enough. From now
on, I'll be mad.

As we step free of the hormonal daydream we entered at puberty, we're no longer limited by our culture's characterization of us as primarily sex objects and childbearers. We're free to define ourselves in our own terms. We are women of substance, and it's our sense of ourselves as more intriguing, more exhilarating, more interesting as we mature that makes this a reality. It's a matter of appreciating our hard-won wisdom, ease, self-confidence, and serenity and celebrating it.

Chapter 5

DON'T WANT NOTHIN' BUT THE REAL THING, BABY

Love consists in this, that two solitudes protect, and border, and salute each other.

—RAINER MARIA RILKE

When we get married or enter into a committed relationship, there are certain unspoken expectations that hide behind our proclamations of love. These are the things that we expect, even demand, from our beloved but would be too embarrassed to admit, let alone say. But they exist nevertheless: I expect you to protect and care for me. I expect you to make me the center of your life. I expect you to be a mind reader, to anticipate my every need and to put me first always. I expect you to be strong, competent, and brave, yet sensitive and attentive. I expect you to heal all my childhood wounds, to adore me, and to make me feel special. I expect you to fulfill me, to give my life meaning, and to make me whole. Quite a tall order. Ridiculous, in fact. But when you stop and think about it, isn't that what you wanted, even counted on, from your mate? Someone who would give you the unconditional love and protection you longed for as a child.

When we fell in love, what we were looking for was an ideal parent, except one with whom there was sexual passion. No, this isn't what we were thinking about when we met our Prince Charming, but on an unconscious level, that was the fantasy. That's the basis of romantic love. It's fostered by hormones, illusions, and infantile longings.

At midlife, many relationships collapse under the burden of these impossible expectations. We can't maintain the fantasy anymore. We know too much. But many of us still long for this dream of being "perfectly met." Yet until we give up this longing, it will continue to interfere with our ability to experience authentic, mature intimacy.

In the pressure cooker of midlife, change in relationships is inevitable. Separation, divorce, affairs occur at various times throughout our lives, but they occur more frequently during this period. They often become the spark that fuels personal transformation. Even if there is no extramarital affair or divorce, many long-term relationships succumb to boredom and deadness.

With children almost grown, having attained financial independence, many women often question whether to remain in their marriage. If the relationship doesn't meet enough of their expectations, if they don't feel that their mate shares enough of their interests and values, if there's a lack of genuine affection and love, women often ask themselves, Why not leave? Why not take a chance and seek a new relationship in which there is more equality and emotional satisfaction or find fulfillment on my own?

Yet there are women, much like many women of our mothers' generation, who decide that it's too big a risk. These women renegotiate the marital contract, but only with themselves. They lower their expectations and re-sign themselves to "simply making the best of it." In other words, they settle. They withdraw from their hus-bands, at least sexually and emotionally, and enter into a marriage of convenience. They throw themselves into ca-reer, other interests, friendships, their children to fulfill the lack in their marriage. They make a life of their own while remaining within a marriage that exists in name only.

Without reevaluation, the midlife relationship is doomed, especially if it interferes with either partner's growth and development. It's not uncommon for a woman to feel the need for something more from her relationship. As she becomes more aware of her own needs, she often feels dissatisfied with the patterns she and her partner may have fallen into. This was the case with the couple you are about to meet.

Mandy and Phil have been married for twenty-six years. They met when Mandy was twenty-five. It was love at first sight. They have two sons, ages twenty and twenty-four. In a recent photograph taken during a family vaca-tion, Phil can be seen waving his walking stick while Mandy—an attractive, heavyset woman with straight shoulder-length auburn hair and large brown eyes—beams with pride as she hugs their sons. The family was tri-umphant after having made the strenuous climb to Chilnualna Falls in Yosemite.

Mandy is soft-spoken. To people who don't know her well, she would be considered shy. She rarely expresses her opinion, often deferring to her gregarious husband. While Phil thrives on being in the spotlight, Mandy seems more than happy to remain in his shadow, even though she's more than his intellectual match.

When Mandy and Phil first met, she had just graduated at the top of her nursing school class. At the time, Mandy had planned to go on to get her master's degree, but she married Phil and became pregnant with their first child. With two young children, Mandy put her career on hold to become a full-time wife and mother.

Phil made his way up the corporate ladder to become the executive vice president of a computer-software firm. Phil's work required that he travel several times a week. This left Mandy with the responsibilities for raising their sons and managing the household. She was a devoted wife and mother, making sure the freezer was stocked with garden burgers when her younger son suddenly announced he was a vegetarian, packing snacks in Phil's bag when he traveled so he'd have food if he arrived at the hotel late, spending hours soliciting ads for the boy's baseball awards book, switching to a Pritikin diet when Phil discovered that he had high cholesterol.

As the children left home for college, Mandy talked to Phil about doing more together, but he was involved in his career and didn't feel the same need. The more they talked, the clearer it became that Phil had a different idea of what made for a good relationship. Mandy grew increasingly frustrated and finally decided to pursue her career full-time. She'd been hired to administer a foundation for degenerative eye diseases, and within a year, she was promoted to executive director.

With her children grown, Mandy had begun to shift the way she was thinking about herself—about what was more important to her and what she wanted out of a relationship. Like many women, Mandy went through a period of self-examination, in which she realized that she'd done all of the compromising in her marriage. She felt both disillusioned and resentful. Our culture's conditioning of women to be selfless makes it difficult for them to express their needs without feeling guilty and selfish. Carol Gilligan coined a phrase that describes a woman's concern for the feelings of others, even at her own expense, as the "ethics of care." Society expects women to put the needs of others before their own. Most women are not only comfortable with this idea but have become experts. In fact, our culture holds selflessness as the standard of feminine goodness.

During midlife, as women experience the pull to attend to their own needs, they often feel conflicted. Much of our value as women has come from our ability to know what others need. It's one of our talents as women. When we begin to bring ourselves back into the equation, it often feels as if we're violating a fundamental rule of femininity—a woman must always put other people's needs before her own. But this condemns us to an impossible ideal. Yet we often wrestle with whether we have a right to put our needs first. We worry that we'll inadvertently cause other people to suffer. As we put more of ourselves into the picture, our essential sense of ourselves often comes into question. We're forced to readjust our internal image to include a woman who sometimes puts her own interests and desires first. For many women, this is a radical shift.

For all of Mandy and Phil's married life, Phil's family had come to their house to celebrate special occasions. Mandy made Thanksgiving as well as Christmas and Easter dinners. She had her in-laws over for birthdays and, on occasion, for Sunday dinner. While her children were young, it was something she did without question. But as they got older, she had mixed feelings. On the one hand, it was important for the children to have a sense of family and tradition; on the other, she resented the responsibility. But she never voiced her frustration. Over the years, it became something that was expected of her.

This year, with her sons going to their respective girlfriends' houses, Mandy decided that she wanted to do something different. Having already hosted Thanksgiving and Christmas, she wanted to go away for Easter. "I'm tired of doing it all myself," Mandy said to me one afternoon. "It takes me three days to get ready for dinner. I want a holiday that's a holiday for me, rather than a holiday for everyone else. I want a break in tradition because the traditions aren't always fun."

Mandy found herself rehearsing what she would say to Phil, until one evening, while they were watching television, she couldn't contain it any longer. "Phil, I'm not having your mom and dad for Easter this year. I just don't want to do the whole thing," she continued, monitoring his reaction. "The ham, the kielbasa, scalloped potatoes, creamed onions, and colored eggs. Why can't somebody else do it for a change? Why is it always on me? The kids aren't going to be here. Let's go to Yosemite for the long weekend."

There was silence. Then Phil tried to convince Mandy to have Easter as usual and to go away the following weekend. They got into a fight, and he accused her of being selfish and insensitive. He told her that she'd changed and that she wasn't the woman he'd married. While Phil's reaction shocked Mandy, she was adamant. She wasn't going to allow her guilt or Phil to deter her. The argument raged on for the next several days. But when Phil finally realized that she was committed, he insisted that she tell the family, which she did. Mandy was discovering an inner strength by listening to her own voice and asserting herself in a way she hadn't previously in her marriage. But as a woman begins to become more vocal, it often upsets the power balance in the relationship.

After Mandy talked to Phil's family, things seemed to settle down. As had been the case throughout their marriage, Mandy tried to talk with Phil, but the conversation went nowhere. She was hopeful that some time alone together might make a difference.

But on the drive up to the cabin they had rented, Phil listened to the radio the entire time. And throughout the weekend, Mandy found it difficult to talk with him. Given how gregarious he was in public, she was taken aback by his remoteness when just the two of them were together. She realized that a lot of the fun and enjoyment they had once shared was missing. There was no playfulness. While she had been vaguely aware of this for a while, being on vacation together made it more apparent. Mandy realized that she experienced more intimacy with her friends and counted more on them for emotional support than on her husband. She was shocked at herself. She began to wonder if she wanted to remain in the relationship.

It was then that I met Mandy. She came to my office dressed in a beige suit and a creamy angora sweater. The effect was smartly professional yet sexy. Her stylish tortoiseshell glasses accentuated her reddish hair. As she sat on the couch, she looked around for a tissue, as if preparing herself for the emotions that were to come. "I thought we had a pretty good marriage," Mandy began. "No, it isn't perfect, but I love my husband. I had this fantasy that with the kids out of the house, we could rediscover each other. But was I in la-la land. Phil works as much as, if not more than, ever. Now that I have a career, he seems resentful. When I refused to have his family over for Easter, he said that I'd changed. It's funny—one of the things he seemed to appreciate when we first got together, my independence, he now complains about.

"I have changed, but not in the ways he thinks. Maybe that's part of the problem. I've changed and he hasn't. I want a partner. I want someone who's as interested in me and my life as I am in his. When I think about it, Phil's not the man I fell in love with. Sure, I wanted someone who would be successful, but not a workaholic. I miss the companionship. It's been a long time since I really felt intimate with Phil." Mandy was clearly frustrated, but her heart was still in her marriage. She didn't want to make a rash decision. Yet at the same time, she felt an urgent need for the relationship to expand and change. Mandy and I talked about the necessity that often occurs in long-term marriages to rebalance the relationship, so that each person's needs are more equally considered. I explained to Mandy that feelings of dissatisfaction and disillusionment were common, especially as women enter midlife and often become more vocal. More often than not, it's the woman who has to initiate the change.

A Couple's Crisis

I asked Mandy what had attracted her to Phil when they first met. She sat silently for several moments as tears welled in her eyes. I had the feeling that she was sorting through every interaction she and her husband had ever had. Then she met my gaze. "I think the first thing about Phil was his warm smile and his sense of humor. He had this wicked, irreverent sense of humor that would make me laugh," she said wistfully. "He's tall and athletic and being with him made me feel safe. He was my prince. I really thought that I'd found my prince. I was gaga."

Mandy was silent for a few moments. It was as if she were looking into the past they'd shared. Then she added, "Phil's very decisive, not like me, or at least not like I used to be. I would take forever to make a decision, whereas he could decide on the spot. He's bright. He has this ency-clopedic kind of knowledge. It's hard for me to believe, but when we were first together, we used to stay up all night and just talk. Sometimes it was about politics or philosophy; sometimes we'd read each other our favorite poems."

Phil was the kind of man Mandy knew would work hard and be successful. He had been a good provider and that had been something that was important to her. "But he's turned into a workaholic. It feels like he's missing in ac-tion. I'm mad as hell at him for leaving me."

I asked Mandy what she meant. "He's just not available. He never talks about anything he's feeling. He mostly reports on what he did at work, if that. It's almost like the man I knew and loved was snatched, and he's been replaced by this serious, stuffy old businessman. I miss the man I married. I'm a bit scared to admit this, but if we can't find a way to connect, if he's not willing to be an equal partner, I don't know if I want this anymore."

Then I asked Mandy what she thought Phil had found attractive in her. Without any hesitation she replied, "That's easy. He used to call me his 'angel with a brain.' I think Phil was drawn to my softness, my nurturing. I think he loved the fact that I looked up to him and thought he was wonderful. I was always very supportive of his dreams and goals. I believed in him. But he also liked the fact that I had a mind of my own. But now that I've worked my way out of the angel business, he's pissed. It feels like he wanted me to have stayed frozen in time and I've thawed out and moved on."

Like Mandy and Phil, we project the parts of ourselves that are the least developed onto our partner. We fall in love when we meet a man who appears to represent everything we're not. We make him into our Prince Charming by imagining that he is powerful, confident, successful, intellectual, decisive—all the aspects of our personality that we've neglected or disowned. We feel certain that in partnership, we'll be complete. In Mandy's case, she was relatively passive when she met Phil. She was attracted to a man who was assertive, expressive, determined, and strong. She admired these qualities in him because she felt that they were missing in her. Ironically, what we once found most attractive in a partner often becomes the thing we find irritating if we don't reclaim the rejected parts of ourselves.

As Mandy rediscovered her own ability to manage her life, she no longer needed Phil to carry those unrealized aspects of her personality. The qualities that she once found appealing in her husband were no longer as attractive. Mandy no longer needed a protector and a provider. She needed a partner—a man who could accept her as his equal. But Phil had continued to allow Mandy to carry his vulnerable, tender side. Throughout their marriage, he relied on Mandy to support and nurture him. The things she had once devoted her life to had changed. But Phil had been so caught up in his career that he hadn't noticed. This created a crisis in their marriage. To a great extent, Phil would have liked the status quo to have remained in place. Yet if their marriage was going to survive, he, too, had to begin to accept Mandy for who she had become. He, too, had to reown those qualities in his personality that he had depended on his wife to express for him.

This isn't an uncommon story for midlife women—children launched or needing less attention, dreams and desires reemerging. In my private practice, I see women facing these issues every day, each struggling to rebalance the needs of others with her own, each trying to change a fundamental inequality in her relationship with her partner.

Shifting the Balance of Power

Our culture fosters a basic inequality between men and women. Mandy realized that on an unconscious level she thought that women were inferior to men. She'd spent much of her married life bolstering Phil instead of attending to herself. While many women have relationships that have far more equality than those of their mother's generation, there's often, nevertheless, the push for greater parity at midlife. Like many women, Mandy now wanted a mate who would share and support her dreams as much as she had supported his. She wanted someone who would share his vulnerability, fears, and insecurities as she did with him. She wanted a companion, friend—a playmate with whom she could share interests and activities. She wanted a partner who would be more involved with her and their children, even though they were now away at college. She wanted someone who would assume more responsibility for running the household.

Like Mandy, many of us do it all—we maintain a career, raise a family, and care for a spouse. But this imbalance interferes with our experiencing genuine intimacy. As is often the case in long-term relationships, the power balance in the marriage has to shift to allow for both partners' feelings and needs. For the first time in her married life, Mandy was struggling to find a new balance in her relationship.

The next time I saw Mandy, she was dressed in jeans, running shoes, and a sweatshirt that was covered in petroglyphs. She sat down on the couch and asked if she could tell me a dream she had had the night before. "I hardly ever remember my dreams, but this one stayed with me," she said. "A little girl is sitting alone in a room. She's all wrapped up like a mummy. A woman walks over to her and puts a hand under her nose to see if she's breathing. At first, she thinks that the little girl is dead, but then she realizes that she's just sleeping. The woman begins to unwrap the girl from the feet up, letting the cloth drop onto the floor. When she reaches her mouth, she hesitates. She's not sure she wants to unwrap the rest of the cloth."

I asked Mandy what she thought her dream meant. "Could it be that I'm that girl?" she asked. "Maybe I've been asleep and I'm starting to wake up. But what about not wanting to unwrap the mouth?"

I asked Mandy how she felt about expressing her own needs to Phil. "It's scary," she replied. "I've spent so much of our marriage going along with the program that I'm afraid of what his reaction will be when I tell him what I want. You know how he reacted when I told him I didn't want to do Easter. Well, that's nothing compared to what I'm thinking now."

I asked her what she thought the girl would say if her mouth was unwrapped. Mandy sat quietly for a moment, looking down at her hands, "I think she'd say, 'I want a full-time husband and partner.' I want to be able to talk to Phil about things that really matter. I'm tired of feeling alone in our marriage. I used to think that once Phil became successful, he'd cut back at work. I lived on that hope for years. But it never happened. I can't live like this anymore. I think I would say, 'Either you commit to making a change and really start to invest yourself in our relationship or leave.'" Mandy was ready to push for a change in spite of her fear. She could no longer tolerate living in a less than satisfying relationship. Mandy and I discussed how to present the situation to Phil.

Women often become more assertive at midlife because they've gained a clearer sense of what they want and feel and are more able to trust themselves. For some women, introducing this newfound sense of power into their marriage may go smoothly. But for others, this change can be extremely difficult.

Renegotiating the Marriage Contract

In order for their marriage to survive, Mandy and Phil had not only to rediscover each other but also to find new ways of being together. They had to adjust the roles, rules, and expectations that had served them over the past twenty-six years to suit both partners' current lives. They had to renegotiate their unspoken contract—that Phil would be a good provider and Mandy would be the nurturer. For years, they had complemented each other, but now the arrangement was unraveling. Mandy was no longer willing to play her part. When one partner refuses to keep up his or her side of the bargain, the other person often decides to leave and look for a new mate. He or she doesn't want to do the work required to change their basic agreement. But marriages can survive this restructuring if both people are willing to renegotiate the terms of the relationship.

Psychoanalyst Roger Gould discusses the benefits for those people who choose to rework their relationship:

> The old conspiracies are abandoned. In their place is a relationship based on empathic acceptance of our authentic partner, who is not a myth, not a god, not a mother, not a father, not a protector, not a censor. Instead there is just another human being with a full range of passions, rational ability, strengths, weaknesses, trying to figure out how to conduct a meaningful life with real friendship and companionship. From this new dynamic, many different forms of marriage may follow: two very separate lives, in which husband and wife come together only periodically, as their rhythm of relating dictates; total sharing of one

life in work and leisure; or variations between these two extremes. In any case it is a relationship of equals, without rank, position or self-abrogation.

It was raining when Mandy arrived for her session. She set her umbrella next to the door, brushed off her gray suit, and settled onto the couch. "I talked with Phil," she began. "At first, he did his usual thing and got defensive. He didn't think that anything was wrong. But when I told him that I thought our marriage was in real trouble, he was shocked. I told him that I couldn't continue to live with the loneliness anymore. He had no idea I felt that way. It's kind of amazing, because I've been talking to him for at least a year now, but I guess my taking a stronger stand made the difference. When I told him that something had to change or I wanted out, he flipped."

Mandy talked with Phil about the fact that she knew their life could be better, that she loved him and thought that he loved her. She emphasized the importance of their shared history and the solid foundation they had, but she said that it seemed as if they were living more as roommates than as husband and wife.

"We got into a huge fight," Mandy continued. "Phil slept in Danny's old room. But as upsetting as it was, it felt better in a way than being ignored. At least we each said what was on our minds. But I couldn't sleep. I was worried that my marriage might be over. I had told him that if he would make a commitment, I was willing to work on the relationship but that we had to get help. I made it clear that that was nonnegotiable.

"The next morning, Phil came into the kitchen. He looked awful. He'd been up all night, too. He said that he felt all torn up inside. He told me that while he resented my demands, he didn't want to lose me or his family. I burst out crying. I really hadn't been sure he'd come around. I was so relieved. This was the first time that I felt he'd really taken me seriously. I knew that we had a lot of work ahead of us, but at least he wanted to make a go of it."

I had given Mandy the name of a couples counselor. With some reluctance, Phil agreed to leave work early so that they could begin therapy.

Like Mandy, many women are surprised at how much power they actually have. While change can threaten the stability of the relationship, it can also provide an opportunity for renewal. But both partners must be willing to do the hard work. This requires that each person look behind the facade and accept the other person for who they are rather than who they wanted them to be. Each partner must come to terms with what the relationship can realistically provide.

Stumbling Toward Intimacy

Shortly after Mandy and Phil began couples therapy, Phil's father had to be admitted to a nursing home. Facing his father's mortality caused Phil to open up to Mandy. As Phil began to spend more time with his father, he saw a man who had been rigid, controlling, self-centered, emotionally distant from his children and wife, a man who had few interests outside his career. Although Phil had always thought of himself as different, he was now horrified by some of their similarities. The vulnerability and dependency he had fought against most of his adult life now began to surface.

Over the next several months, Mandy talked about the change in Phil. "I guess it's a combination of things, but there's hope. There's definitely hope. Since his father's health has gone downhill, Phil's become more available. We've had some wonderful talks. One night, he actually cried in my arms. I can't believe this guy. You think that after being married to a person for all these years you know them, but you really don't. I think a big part of it was that we kind of took each other for granted and fell into a rut. Not having any methods for real communication didn't help, either. But as we work on the relationship, we're learning a lot about each other.

"I've made some pretty radical changes at home," Mandy continued. "June Cleaver threw down her apron and stopped cooking. Amazingly, no one seems to have died. In fact, Phil doesn't seem to mind a bit. I cook when inspiration strikes, but mostly either I pick up takeout on the way home from work or Phil will call from the office and ask what I want for dinner. He's gotten a lot easier about divvying up the household responsibilities. It's not all on me anymore. He's even started to do some of the grocery shopping, and he seems to like it. I'm blown away. There's been a big shift for both of us. We've reached a place which I wish we'd been able to get to earlier in our marriage."

Mandy and Phil had let go of the unrealistic expectations they had unknowingly brought into their marriage. They'd reached a point where they accepted each other for who they are. Over time, we must come to accept that our knight in shining armor is merely human, with limitations, needs, and longings similar to our own. We must withdraw our projections in order to discover genuine intimacy.

"Instead of thinking about what I might have with the perfect man, I've become more present with Phil," Mandy explained. "I think I had a fantasy that there was someone out there who was going to be my ideal match and would make me happy. I gave that up. I came to the conclusion that no one was going to care as much about my life as I do. And that it wasn't up to Phil to fulfill me. I had to do it myself. That was a big one."

In our intimate relationships, we can care for and encourage one another, but each partner must be responsible for herself or himself. We can't rely on a partner to live out the undeveloped aspects of our personalities. One of the essential tasks of midlife is to assume responsibility for our own growth and happiness. However, one of the wonderful dimensions of a relationship is that our partners introduce us to interests, ideas, and activities we may not have been drawn to on our own. A mate offers us a different perspective on ourselves and the world. In this way, a mate enlarges and enriches our lives and contributes to our happiness. But if we rely too heavily on a partner for our fulfillment, the relationship becomes fundamentally crippled.

"Since doing couples therapy, we've realized that we're on the same team. We've gotten a lighter attitude about handling things, and Phil's wicked sense of humor has returned. It really helps." As Phil experienced this transformation, he cut back at work and rekindled an interest that he'd let go of years earlier—racing road cars at a track and instructing. "He loves it," Mandy reported. "The intensity is pretty equal to his work, and it's brought a balance into his life that was missing. We're each doing our own things, but now we come together for what we need with each other. If you had asked me a year ago if I thought this was possible, I would've said no way. But I actually have a real marriage."

As writer Anne Morrow Lindbergh wrote, "In a growing relationship, the original essence is not lost but merely buried under the impedimenta of life. The core of reality is still there and needs only to be increased and reaffirmed."

This was certainly true of Mandy and Phil. While they were now more comfortable pursuing parts of their lives separately, the level of intimacy and equality had increased. Mandy had taken a risk. She was secure enough that she wasn't willing to settle for a compromised relationship. Had she not challenged Phil to change, it's more than likely that he would have remained in his unfulfilling rut.

The word *intimacy* is derived from the Greek *intimare*, which means "inmost, deepest, most profound or close friendship." At midlife, our relationships are more closely akin to a deep, abiding friendship than they are to the raging, tumultuous passion of our youth. No, this doesn't mean that we can't still experience passion. But it will no longer be based on the fantasy that we've discovered our perfect Prince Charming or are going to be rescued.

Truthfully, if you had to choose between a white-hot romance or a deeply intimate partnership, which would you choose? I know, some of you are asking, Well, how white-hot? Just how long do you think it could last? How bad would the breakup be? But all kidding aside, what most women I speak to want, at this stage of their lives, is an authentic, mature love—a love that is based on appreciation, affection, mutual respect, and equality. This kind of intimacy is only possible when we assume greater responsibility for our own growth. As we do so, our relationships become less dependent.

Part of the work of midlife is for us to become more fully integrated. Despite the fact that many of us have had careers throughout the first half of our lives, we often sought a sense of wholeness through our intimate relationships. At midlife, we can no longer try to attain this sense of completion through another person. We can no longer vicariously live out parts of our lives through someone else. Our authentic self demands that we own all of who we are—our strength, playfulness, intelligence, creativity, assertiveness—any of the qualities we allowed someone else to express for us. At midlife, we must give our neglected parts expression and become more fully ourselves. While some women are able to do this within a relationship, there are others who have either chosen or have been forced to do the work of integration on their own.

Only Grown-ups Need Apply!

It was a crisp fall afternoon. There wasn't a cloud in the sky. A hint of wood smoke drifted through the air. The sidewalk to the Children's Museum was blanketed in golden leaves, which made a rustling sound as the women entered the building. This was not the regular women's group, but a special meeting for singles only. The women nestled into a pile of large kilim pillows in a cozy carpeted room. It brought back memories of when we were pre-teens and would congregate behind closed doors to talk about forbidden subjects. Only now we were grown up and gathered to talk about being single in midlife.

Two of the women were from the women's group, but there were three new participants. I began by asking each woman to introduce herself, give her age, and tell how she had arrived at being single at midlife and how she felt about it. Cynthia, a fifty-six-year-old urban planner, broke the ice. "I'd been married to Adam for twenty-two years, and it's been almost three years since my divorce. It was a struggle at first. It was the first time in my entire life that I'd been alone. When I first got divorced, I was terrified. Truthfully, I didn't think I could make a life for myself. But after a year, I began to feel truly liberated."

Cynthia recalled going to Pier One to buy some plastic glasses for her new house several months after her divorce. She stood at the shelf. There were clear glasses and brightly colored red, blue, and green Mexican tumblers. "My instantaneous thought was I should get the clear glasses because Adam doesn't like color. I was in a trance. I was putting them into my basket when I snapped out of it. I thought, Wait a minute. I don't have to consider Adam anymore. All these years, I've gotten the plain, when I love color. And I put the clear ones back and filled my bas-ket with these outrageous Mexican glasses. I probably bought more than I needed. But the freedom I felt was in-credible. The poor girl at the checkout counter heard far more about me than she ever wanted to know when she said, 'Aren't those great glasses?'" Everyone laughed at what seemed like a simple, everyday incident, but in Cynthia's case, it spoke volumes about the freedom she was feeling.

Joanne, a forty-eight-year-old elementary school teacher, had been married for twenty-six years when her husband died of leukemia three years ago. "There are times I've wondered if I could have gotten my teaching credential, taught sixth grade, and taken classes in computer graphics if Fred had come back," she said. "There are a lot of areas I've grown in since he died, and I'm pleased about that. We'd done everything together, probably too much. It was one of the things we started to talk about before he got sick. I really wanted to do more of my own thing. Well, by George, I've really had to."

As a result of her financial situation, Joanne had to develop some of the land she and Fred had owned. She acknowledged that had her husband still been alive, she would have left the task to him. But having undertaken the project alone, Joanne discovered qualities "I never knew I had, and that feels really good. I have to admit that as much as I miss Fred, I like being my own boss."

Cynthia and Joanne, like so many single women, were experiencing a new sense of independence. While they had not intended to be single at midlife, they were using their considerable resources to create fulfilling, meaningful lives. Cynthia was discovering long-neglected interests, Joanne a mastery that she found invaluable.

For many women, being single at midlife has launched them on a path of self-discovery. The women who had married and raised a family often found that they'd catered to their children and, in many cases, to their husbands. If that was the case, these women are now shaping a life based on what that they want—their own interests, passions, and dreams. In the process, many women discover a new sense of competence and adventure, of which they feel protective.

I'd Love to Be in a Relationship, but Not at Any Price

After an hour of nonstop discussion, we took a short break. When I walked back into the room, several of the women sat rapt in conversation. When I was able to get their attention, I asked how they felt about getting reinvolved with a man. Fran, a fifty-year-old artist, spoke right up. She had been married for seventeen years and divorced for seven. "I would love to be with someone. But I can't compete with young girls. That's not what it's about. Someone's going to have to see me for all the things I am. I want love and respect first and foremost. Then I want a good friend and a lover. Pretty much in that order. I've gotten a lot more picky as I've gotten older. There are so many babies out there that one of my mottoes has become Only grown-ups need apply."

Joanne interjected, "I feel the same. If I'm ever with someone again, I want a man like the priest at my church."

Fran asked, "You mean the gay priest?"

"Well, yes. I know that there are one or two little stumbling blocks. But we could clone him and he'd be perfect. He's a real mensch."

"Mensch?" Cynthia asked, looking puzzled.

"Yeah, it's a Yiddish word," Joanne explained. "It means someone who's honest, responsible, trustworthy. A man with integrity."

Fran said, "You mean a Boy Scout."

"Come to think of it," Joanne responded, "he'd have to have a lot of those kind of qualities. The capacity to be a good friend, but not a prude. By all means, not a prude."

"Well, about six months ago, I thought I'd found someone who fit those qualifications," Fran continued. "I met Alex at the Memorial Day pancake breakfast. He's kind of a manly man, which I really like. This summer, he took a fourteen-day raft trip down the Colorado, and he wants to run the Zambezi next year. So he does neat things. For the first time in a while, I was attracted to someone. Plus, he definitely met the grown-up criteria. So we started to spend time together. I felt really comfortable with him, but I just didn't know about the intelligence thing—if he was smart enough. That was definitely an issue."

After going out on three dates, Alex began to call Fran several times a day. Alex had been successful in business and had retired early.

"At first, it felt really nourishing that he wanted to take care of me. But pretty quickly it felt like too much. I started to think that he needed another hobby besides me. It freaked me out. He was moving way too fast. We talked about it, and it was better for a little while. But I went through a thing where I told him I had to work and couldn't see him. He flipped out. All this neediness came up in him. It was like, I can't do this. You're threatening my independence. He needed a life of his own."

While most single women at midlife would like to be with a man, they have a clearer idea of what they want from a relationship and they aren't willing to give up their hard-won autonomy or settle for less than what they know is possible.

"I started to get down on myself," Fran continued.

"Here was somebody offering me all this stuff that I'd wanted and I was saying no. I wondered if I was just being resistant. Was I too set in my ways? Had I been on my own for so long that I'd become too rigid, and were these issues going to be a deal breaker with anybody? And then I went, No. If I can't trust my instincts, then what the hell else can I trust? And that's what I thought with him. I really, really knew the answer. I didn't want a relationship that would add stress to my life. I just won't settle. So I had 'the talk' with Alex."

Most women feel that unless a man is going to enhance their lives, they have too much to lose by getting involved.

"I'm feeling the same thing," Rita, a fifty-two-year-old lesbian who has a successful career as a research assistant, said. "You'd think it would be easier to meet a woman, but it's not. I'm having a harder time reading the signals. One of the challenges is how to tell if someone's available. It's obvious when a man is interested. But it's not so obvious with a woman. There's more dancing to be done to figure out if that person could be interested."

"How do you meet other women?" Fran asked.

"Yeah, good question," Rita said. "Here you are, walking around in the regular world, and you're looking for those little eye contacts, a lingering hug or other clues. But sometimes that's not anything more than a woman being open and friendly. It's easy to misinterpret the signal. For the most part, I meet women professionally, at church, or sometimes I get fixed up by friends. One time, I got brave and answered an ad in the personals. I'll never do that again. It was so awkward. It's difficult to connect with just the right woman. Actually, it's not that big a deal. I'm pretty happy on my own. But I would like a playmate."

Like so many single women, Joanne and Rita missed companionship the most. What the majority of single women I interviewed wanted was a good friend. Most were surprised to find that their requirements for a lover and those for a close friend had become quite similar.

He May Not Be a Prince, but He's a Real Man!

"Well, I have to admit, I'd kissed more than my share of frogs. In fact, one of my girlfriends had given me a rubber stamp of a frog wearing a crown last Christmas. Honey, I've kissed so many that my lips were getting chapped," Carol, a forty-seven-year-old psychiatric social worker, said. "I didn't want to waste my time anymore. I simply stopped looking. I've been single for ten years. I have a career I love. I play tennis, I have lots of friends, and I just started watercolor classes. The only thing that would've put the icing on the cake would have been to have a wonderful man in my life. But after years of going out with men who barely had a pulse, who wanted a mom or an audience, I thought all the good ones were already taken. Then this amazing thing happened." Carol had been traveling back from her mother's eightieth birthday party. Her flight had been canceled and she was rebooked on another airline. "I was sitting in the waiting area when I saw this man and woman walk by. I thought, He's cute," she said. "He boarded the plane, and as I was walking down the aisle, we caught each other's eye. When I found my seat, it was across the aisle from him. As I sat down, we started to talk. He was supposed to be planning for a business meeting with the woman next to him. But instead, we talked for the entire flight.

"By the time we landed, I asked him if he wanted to go to the Eagles concert. He had a business meeting and couldn't go, but he asked for my phone number. He called the next day and came over. He had made dinner reservations at Pasquals, my favorite restaurant. But we never left the couch. We made out a little and I offered that he could stay in the extra bedroom instead of driving back to Albuquerque. We ended up spending the weekend together."

Monday morning, when it was time for Ted to go back to New Jersey, Carol felt sad and worried. She wondered if he would stay in touch. "He called me every day," she said. "Two weeks later, he flew out. By the time he came back, that was it. We were so connected. We made love, and it was amazing. It was completely different from anything I'd experienced before. In the past, there was a lot of passion and hot sex, but never a feeling of real love. Now there was both. Ted was the kind of guy I had always rejected. He was too solid and healthy. But I knew I didn't want to blow it this time."

In April, after a six-month long-distance relationship, Ted sold his house and moved to Santa Fe. "We've been living together for nine months now. So are you going to kick me out of the group? I guess I'm not exactly single anymore. But I was up until just recently." Everyone laughed. The women were clearly taken with Carol's story.

"So does he have a brother or a friend?" Fran asked, only half-joking.

Most of the single women I interviewed would like to have a man in their lives, but it no longer feels essential. For those women who have never married, they've already created a life of their own. For women who had at one time been married or in a long-term relationship, at midlife they're no longer looking for a man to give their lives meaning or to define them. These women aren't willing to compromise their quality of life simply to be with a man. They are creating their lives based on their own needs and dreams. At this stage of life, they want both intimacy and freedom.

The Best of Both Worlds

Several women I interviewed expressed concern about being able to maintain their center if they got involved in a new relationship. As committed as they were to living their own lives, they worried that their old inclinations would kick in and they would focus too much attention on a man. They knew themselves well enough to know that they were still susceptible to being "swept away."

For many women, a crucial aspect of creating a solid midlife relationship is making sure that there are physical and emotional boundaries. Many expressed a need to build in safeguards—a way to protect them against "relationship meltdown." Some women create these boundaries by maintaining separate households; some place limits on the amount of time they're available; others have relationships with men who live in a different city or country.

Cynthia boasted, "Ladies, I think I've figured out how to have the best of both worlds." The women leaned forward, eager to hear Cynthia's secret. "From the time of my first divorce, I swore I'd never be financially dependent on anybody again. And I'm not. It was really important to me that I not get into another relationship where I was going to lose myself. I created this wonderful life for myself, but one thing was missing. I missed having a companion."

Two years ago, Cynthia was at a conference in London. She met a man, and they began to see each other. "I have no desire to get remarried or even to live with anybody again. Which is great, because he's European. We don't see each other as frequently as if he were living in the States. We talk once a week, sometimes more, and we see each other on average once every five or six weeks. My company has an apartment in New York, so either he comes there or we meet in Paris. It's intimacy at a distance.

"My career is very demanding, and I have a large network of friends, so this relationship allows me to have a wonderful playmate and lover while maintaining my independence. It's absolutely terrific. He's given me a whole new ability to live for the day, because there's no traditional future in this relationship."

"Sounds like something out of a movie," Joanne commented. "I always thought that Katharine Hepburn was very smart. She had a lover, but they had separate households. That way, you can wake up in the morning, and nobody's there to ask why you're not bright and cheery or why the coffee isn't made. I can see the pluses of living alone and having a lover and companion."

Women who choose to build boundaries into their relationships find that they can maintain "a life of their own" while enjoying companionship and sexual and emotional intimacy. While there may be some inherent limitations to these types of relationships, they afford women companionship and affection while protecting their independence and time.

The need to be in a relationship seems to be an inherent part of being human. Whether you're single or in a long-term marriage, one of the essential challenges of midlife involves giving up "the Dream." You know, the Dream of the "perfect love" or the "perfect partner." The dream that your prince will discover you asleep in the forest and will kiss you back to life. Regardless of our marital status, we can't waste any more of our precious time waiting. We must become our own prince and kiss ourselves awake. We can no longer rely on anyone, not even a devoted partner, for what we most deeply want and need. It's time to assume responsibility for our lives and create the fulfillment we long for.

I hope I'm not the first to break the news to you. But, in truth, the Dream never existed. It was assembled out of the vague, vaporous fantasies of youth. Just as our other illusions stand in the way of our experiencing maturity, the Dream stands in the way of our finding genuine intimacy.

Authentic intimacy requires that we accept the fact that all we can realistically hope for are imperfect connections—connections with other flawed, limited, unique, wonderful human beings; in which we can see and be seen, know and be known; in which we experience enough trust that we can reveal our innermost selves to another. For those of us in a relationship, that connection may be with our mate. For those of us who are single, it may be with a cherished friend. But regardless of what form our intimate connections take, they become more essential as we navigate this midlife passage.

Chapter 6

GROWING UP ISN'T FOR SISSIES

It's life's illusions I recall / I really don't know life at all.

—JONI MITCHELL

I know, you're probably saying to yourself, Why is she talking about growing up? I left home eons ago. I have a responsible job. I pay my bills. I've raised a family. I live my own life, make my own decisions. I've been a grown-up for years. Although you may be an adult, chronologically and intellectually few of us have left home completely. Leaving home is a process that is done in steps. Undoubtedly, you have laid a lot of the essential groundwork. For most of us, though, there's still a significant amount of internal work to be done. I don't want to imply that you haven't worked for all that you've accomplished. But constructing the outer manifestation of adulthood is relatively easy compared to the complex inner work of growing up emotionally.

I realize these statements may sound ludicrous. But consider for a moment whether, on a subliminal level, you still subscribe to at least some of these cherished assumptions: I have control over my life. If I play by my parents' rules, do everything right, and work really hard, things will work out. But if I get tired, confused, or am unable, my parents will step in to rescue me. Life is understandable. If I'm a "good girl," I'll be exempt from the misfortunes that befall ordinary people.

In order to become a bona fide adult, rather than one who is simply gold-plated, we must disentangle ourselves from the web of illusions that lie just below the surface of our awareness. Although those illusions provided a sense of comfort and protection when we were children and even young adults, if we don't dismantle them, we will remain prisoners of childhood, regardless of how successful our lives may appear. We must give up the futile search for the security, trust, and unconditional love we longed for as children.

The residual helplessness and dependency prevent us from ever feeling truly grown-up. Without realizing it, our childhood beliefs are like imaginary parents. They require our blind obedience. As long as we try to remain within the boundaries of what our parents defined as legitimate and acceptable, we're under someone else's influence and our life is not our own. Our false assumptions interfere with a deeper connection with our authentic self.

The Message of Impermanence

It seems that overnight, people our age are getting cancer and having heart attacks. Worse yet, most of us have friends our age who have died. In every ache and pain, in our changing energy level, in our changing roles with our parents and children, we catch glimpses of our own mortality.

When a parent dies, our world is turned upside down—we feel scared, shaken. We've lost our buffer. We're next in line. Life as we have known it has been transformed. Even if our parents are still alive, we see their frailty. They want us to drive, to talk with their doctor. We're concerned about their health, their finances. Suddenly, we have become the parent—their caretakers. We can no longer maintain the illusion that our parents will always protect us.

As children, when we had a nightmare or were frightened, we called our parents to allay our fears. They would come into our room and show us that there were no monsters in the closet, or we would crawl into their bed and find comfort in the warmth of their bodies. In either case, they reassured us. As a result, we endowed our parents with magical power. They were the ones who would take care of us. They were the ones who knew about the world. Although we know better, the fantasy continues into our adult lives.

But what happens when we're confronted with our own mortality? And no one—not our parents, partners, clergy—has the power to make that dread go away. What happens when we are faced with the stark fact that there are certain things in life that must be faced head-on and no one can save us from them? Another sliver of reality creeps in and further shakes our already-tenuous illusions. This all adds up to the unmistakable reminder that we are now the ones doing the caring and protecting, not only for our parents and children but ultimately for ourselves, as well.

Despite how we may feel, we must be prepared to accept a fact that we have desperately tried to avoid all our lives: We are separate, alone. With this realization, our innocence is gone forever. We can no longer pretend that we're immortal, that an all-powerful being is going to rescue us. The truth is that we are vulnerable. We are now the authorities.

While this realization can be frightening, at least initially, the paradox is that as we become more aware of our own finiteness, we experience greater depth and understanding. We discover a longing to be alive. As author Elisabeth Kübler-Ross reminds us, "It's only when we truly know and understand that we have a limited time on earth—and that we have no way of knowing when our time is up—that we will begin to live each day to the fullest, as if it was the only one we had."

Our recognition of death can take many forms. We experience a small death when a child leaves home, when we lose our job, experience an illness, or go through a divorce. These situations make us aware of just how vulnerable we are, that no one can save or protect us—not our spouse, our children, not wealth. While we find comfort in the love of our family and in financial security, they can't shield us from the harsh realities of life. Each time we experience a loss, there's a disillusionment—life isn't what we thought and another veil is ripped from our childhood fantasy.

Loss, however, leads to growth. Once we realize that we are "the one"—that whatever we're going to make of our lives rests completely in our hands—we become energized. We can no longer pretend that our choices are unlimited. The realization that our time is finite forces us to decide what's important in life.

Once Upon a Time: The Promise of Love and Protection

As children, we begin life helpless. Because of our dependency, we believe in the omnipotence of our parents. No matter what the reality, we idealize them. While both parents play an important role in our development, a little girl's first protector and model is her mother. From the time we were pip-squeaks and our mothers towered over us, we wanted to be like them. To be like one's mother meant being safe.

As we grew older and explored the world, our parents continued to guide and defend us. They taught us not to go near the hot stove, not to run into the street, not to play on the stairs. After hearing our mothers' repeated cautions, we internalized these warnings and eventually made them our own. Our mother's voice is always inside each of us. It becomes our guardian angel—ever present, ever watchful—keeping us out of harm's way. We have the fantasy that our parents are always here to look out for us. But the reality is that we are protected because we adopted their values, beliefs, and rules. That's how we survived. But that internal voice also interferes with our freedom—we must obey it in order to remain within our parents' sphere of influence.

For most women, a mother's internalized voice is often the loudest. But at some point, we had to test our own capabilities. We had to find out if we could go near the stove without getting burned, if we could cross the street without being run over, if we could climb the stairs and not get hurt. We needed to know that we could navigate the larger world successfully.

As we accumulated experiences in which we relied on

our own judgment, our sense of authority gradually shifted away from our internal parent toward our selves. Each time we were successful, our trust of ourselves grew. But the internalized voice of one's mother remains. Whenever we step outside what she considered acceptable, we hear from her: "Are you sure it's a good idea to have a child this late in life?" "Do you think it's wise to risk your financial security by going after your dream?" "Aren't you going to jeopardize your marriage by making so many demands on your husband?" And the litany goes on.

The Power of Illusions

The process of unearthing and challenging our childhood assumptions takes a lifetime. At every stage of growth, we move forward and then falter; we grow and then retreat. With each transition, we must let go of some of our illusions of safety. What was appropriate for one stage may be constricting at another. We must move step by step away from "childhood consciousness."

Psychoanalyst Roger Gould presented the idea of childhood consciousness in this way:

Our subjective experience of life and our behaviors are governed by literally thousands of beliefs (ideas) that compose the map used for interpreting the events of our life (including our own mental events). When we grow, we correct a belief that has restricted and restrained us unnecessarily. For example, when we learn as young children that there is no universal law requiring us to be what our parents wanted us to be, we are released to explore and experiment. A door to a new level of consciousness is opened.

There is often an enormous gap between our parents' expectations and demands and what we truly want for ourselves. Unfortunately, the unconscious pressure we feel to remain within their imaginary protection often overshadows our own needs and desires. In midlife, when we feel an urgency to pursue our own dreams and longings, we must unearth our childhood assumptions so that they can be dismantled. But our illusions often remain just out of our awareness until something in our lives intervenes to expose them. That's what happened to one of my clients.

Allison walked into my office carrying a Diet Coke. She had divorced her husband a year and a half ago and was now involved with another woman. She was dressed in a pair of khaki cotton pants and a sky blue T-shirt that was covered with a pattern of billowy white clouds. She put her drink on the floor, slipped out of her sandals, and curled her feet under her on the couch. It had been a little over a year since I had last seen her. Her hair was shorter and dyed jet black. Allison had just celebrated her fifty-third birthday by taking a two-week trip to Brazil. She had worked as a hearing officer for the family courts for the past seven and a half years. "I came home from my trip feeling relaxed and rested," she said. "But when I went back to the office, something felt strange. I asked my assistant if anything was going on and he assured me that everything was fine.

"The next day, I was called into the head judge's office. I was told that I had been accused of sexual harassment." She looked into space for a few moments as tears streamed down her cheeks. Then she wiped them away and continued. "I was stunned. It turned out that Tom, one of my assistants, had lodged the complaint. He said that I had made sexual advances toward him. Which is so ridiculous. I couldn't believe it."

Allison was placed on administrative leave while the charges were investigated. She was now waking up in the middle of the night panic-stricken. "Food has always been my drug of choice," she said. "And since this whole thing blew up I haven't been able to eat. I've always prided myself on being fair. I've worked hard to build a good reputation. But all that's in jeopardy now. If they don't let me keep my job, I don't know what I'm going to do. I'm too old to start over."

Allison is the eldest of three children. Her father had worked in a steel mill, but he had abandoned the family when she was seven. Her mother worked in a dress factory and took in sewing and mending. Allison's mother encouraged her, from an early age, to do well in school and to get a college education. The continual message she received from her mother was, "You don't want to end up like me. Make something of yourself. Play by the rules." Her mother longed for stability, which she never had.

Allison went on to receive a law degree. With the exception of a two-year period when she worked on her own, she had spent most of her professional career within the judicial bureaucracy. While she knew that she wasn't using all of her skills and talents, she enjoyed the security that working for a government institution provided. Allison's deeply held belief that if she was a "good girl" everything would work out was now being threatened.

I asked Allison if she had any idea of what might have prompted these charges. "I've been racking my brain trying to think of what made him do this. Yeah, we goofed around and there was some sexual banter, not just between us but with everyone. But that was it. He gave me a glowing midyear review. He said that I was the best supervisor he had ever worked for. When I look back, things changed between us last June. Tom came into work wearing a sleeveless V-necked vest. I told him nicely that I thought it was inappropriate and asked him to go home and change. From that point on, things between us were never the same. I bent over backward for this guy. Now I hate him. I just hate him. I wanted to do something to retaliate. But instead, I put my anger to good use. I stripped the tile on my kitchen counters. I got acid and cleaned all the grunge out of the grout and sealed it so it couldn't grow back. Pretty symbolic, huh?"

The End of Innocence

"I just never in my wildest imagination would have thought this could happen to me," Allison continued. "I did everything right. It makes me wonder about myself. I'm not quite sure how I'm supposed to be in the world. It's really made me wonder whom I can trust. I don't feel like I can trust anyone." We talked about the difference between the blind trust of a child and becoming discerning. She could no longer afford to be indiscriminate.

Allison's sense of herself and her place in the world had been thrown into a state of turmoil. She was questioning everything—the very foundation upon which she had built her life. She felt as if something had died. She was shedding a familiar skin, a skin that had faithfully held and

protected her, a skin she had carefully built up throughout her early adulthood, one that was based on pleasing
others, proving herself, and becoming successful. All of
which she had accomplished. But now, that identity no
longer served her. Allison was in the process of letting go
of a network of assumptions, rules, fantasies, and beliefs.
She had spent much of her life being careful, trying to
follow the rules. But such childhood consciousness was
too limiting for what was longing to emerge. She was
struggling with the death of her old identity. Her innocence had been lost. It was dying in order to allow a fuller,
more mature self to emerge. As Jungian analyst and author Marion Woodman wrote, "Life as we have known it
is over. No longer who we were, we know not who we may
become."

The next time I saw Allison, she seemed uneasy. She
fidgeted with her hair as she spoke. "I got a call to go see
the head judge. My attorney went with me. Before I got
there, I had a bad feeling. Sure enough, I was handed a
bound book with the contents of the investigation. He
told me that the committee had decided to terminate my
services. They gave me the opportunity to continue my
benefits for another eighteen months, so that gives me a bit
of breathing room." Although Allison had three witnesses
who would corroborate her innocence, she decided that she
didn't want to fight the charges. She had been hired as an
"at will employee," which meant that she had no job protection. The judicial review committee could fire Allison
at their discretion. There were, however, strict guidelines
within the court system that guaranteed that no one could
talk about her dismissal. While Allison had been comfortable in her job, she knew that she had been treading

water. Despite the regular paycheck and benefits, Allison no longer wanted to work within the confines of a bureaucracy, especially one in which she could be treated so unjustly.

Nevertheless, Allison couldn't believe that this was happening to her. She had been a model employee. "I keep hearing my mother's voice saying, 'Life's not fair. How many times do I have to tell you? It's just not fair. But you should have been more careful. You should have safeguarded your job.' I guess she was right. I really thought that I'd found my place and that I was secure. And wham, I'm out." Allison sat shaking her head in disbelief. "It's not like I haven't been battered around before, but never like this.

"I woke up at two-thirty last night, wide-awake out of a dead sleep," she said. "I was scared. In my dream, I was in an iron foundry where ore was being smelted down in huge vats into molten steel. That's how I feel, stripped, melted down to my bones. I scurry around inside myself trying to find a trace of the woman in her business suit who was so cocky and self-assured. But she's gone. That part of my life is gone." She paused, then went on. "Now I'm just scared, partly about money. I know I have a cushion. But I keep imagining myself with my computer, phone, and files stuffed in a shopping cart, wandering around town looking for work. I just want my life back. I want things the way they were, damn it! I can't stand feeling like this anymore."

I empathized with the distress Allison was in and how difficult it was to be between worlds. I wanted her to know that she wasn't alone in this struggle. The pull to return to the familiar is universal. Whenever a childhood illusion is attacked by life, we feel anxious and want to return to the way things were. Allison worried about starting a law practice. How would she get clients? How long would it take to build a reputation? What if she went through her savings before she could get established? Allison's tether to her mother and her imaginary protection had been severed. She felt as if life without her illusions would be intolerable. If she couldn't count on what she had relied on, what could she trust? As she was stepping free of her mother's belief system, she was in a state of inner turmoil.

If security means remaining near our parents, it's not surprising that we feel threatened when we make decisions that may contradict their opinions—for example, if we decide to divorce when no one in our family has done so before; if we make our career a major focus in our lives, when our mothers remained at home; if we decide to invest in the stock market against our parents' advice. While Allison had heeded her mother's warnings, they hadn't protected her. The loss of her job had forced her to step beyond her childhood rules.

Each time we assert our independence, it often creates conflict—both with our parents and, more importantly, within ourselves. We don't want to wander too far outside their prescribed boundaries. We all long to return to a place where we felt loved. When times get tough, we want to be able to find shelter and safety under our parents' protective umbrella. This is an issue we wrestle with throughout our lives: How much independence can we tolerate? How much of our lives can we claim for ourselves?

But I'm Not Ready to Be a Grown-up

Anytime we take a risk and step beyond what our inner parent considers safe and acceptable—anytime we challenge ourselves to go beyond what we thought we were capable of and pursue our dreams—fear and anxiety hit us in the face. When Allison thought about opening her own law office, she felt unsure of herself. "I would have been perfectly happy keeping my illusions and having them remain in place until the day I died," she said. "I could have stayed in that job forever. I guess I needed a kick in the butt to move on. I was pretty comfortable, but I can't say I was growing. When I think back on it, there were signs of trouble since June. I guess I just didn't want to see them. I know this is going to sound pathetic coming from a fifty-three-year-old woman, but I don't feel like I have what it takes to stand on my own two feet. I just don't feel prepared."

Despite having been on her own since she was nineteen, and the fact that she was in a relationship, albeit a new one, Allison felt alone for the first time in her life. Her questioning and feelings of insecurity were a natural part of this midlife passage. I reassured Allison that it isn't uncommon to feel the shame of a child when we break a sacred rule in order to follow our own dreams. But where do we find the courage to make room for new possibilities to emerge? If we look back over our lives and recall all the challenges and struggles we have endured, we realize that perhaps we have been selling ourselves short.

I reminded Allison of all that she had survived: working two jobs to put herself through college; surviving her divorce and negotiating an equitable settlement with her ex-husband; raising her son and daughter alone; forging a successful career; caring for her mother, who had Alzheimer's. Before I could go on, she interrupted me. "Okay, there's a part of me that knows I can do it. But there are times when I feel like a helpless little girl. I scurry around trying to think of whom I can run to. But I guess that person would be me. I'm terrified. It doesn't really make sense. As you said, I have managed difficult situations, but somehow, this feels different. What is it?"

In spite of all that she had accomplished, this was the first time that Allison had so clearly unmasked her childhood illusions. She had peeled away another layer of the imaginary buffer that had stood between her and reality. She was stripped down to her essential self and was facing life, not as she imagined or wanted it to be, but as it was. There was a shift in her thinking from magical to realistic. Although few of us would choose the challenges life presents us, when we accept reality and successfully cope with a difficult situation, we gain a greater sense of mastery and maturity. But few of us behave like an adult every single minute of the day. Growing up takes time. But like Allison's, our infantile longings and wishes can undermine our adult goals.

"I've spent so much of my life being careful—trying to make sure that everything would work out. I actually think that I was trying to figure out how to keep myself safe. But I'm sick of it," Allison said. "I did it in my marriage. I made myself and my needs invisible. I tiptoed around my husband and didn't say what I thought and felt a lot of the time. I did the same thing at work. I tried to be a model employee. I think I even did it with my children. I bent over backward to be a perfect mom. I'm tired of being so cautious. I feel like all these rules about how I'm supposed to be have been suffocating me. I want to take a stand for myself for a change, rather than always considering other people first. Besides, it didn't work anyway. I'm caring, I'm kind, I'm considerate, but I don't have to be cautious anymore. At least not in the way I have been. That feels more protective than what I've been doing."

The dismantling of illusions allows room for us to expand our sense of ourselves and what we want from life. All bets are off. The rules we tried so hard to adhere to didn't buy us the protection we longed for. Now it's time to make our own.

Forging a New Adult Identity

With the loss of her job, Allison had been forced to take another step toward maturity. Like most of us, she was not willing to leave the safety of what's familiar until she was pushed. Throughout our lives, we take steps away from childhood toward becoming an adult—leaving home, going to college, getting married, having children, establishing a career. At every stage in our development, we experience loss and anxiety. Rather than interpret these uncomfortable feelings as a sign of failure or that we've done something wrong, we need to see them as an indication of progress—we've moved into uncharted territory.

The next time I saw Allison, she was wearing a pair of black slacks, a green long-sleeved blouse, and a multicolored scarf. The stress that had been written across her face for the past couple of months had been replaced by a sparkle in her eyes. Before she even sat down, she announced, "I've set up my home office. I installed a business phone, got a post office box, and am going to order stationery when I leave here. I've made some calls to colleagues about referrals. I've gotten my first client, and she gave me a large retainer."

I commented that it sounded like she was launched. "Catapulted," she responded. "They did me such a big favor. I can't stop twinkling. I kind of feel like I can do anything now. I didn't realize how much I'd missed being an advocate. I love representing parents and helping them create a workable situation for their children. I've gotten calls from two other potential clients." I remarked that it had only been two months. "I know." Allison beamed.

"I'm giving birth to my own business."

Allison was giving birth to more than a business. She was giving birth to a mature, adult self. She was now freer to attend to what she most valued and believed in. For the first time in her life, she was shaping life on her own terms.

Allison discovered what I think is true for all of us. As we embrace a new sense of responsibility, few of us would want to return to childhood again. It's essential now that we become our own authority; otherwise, the second half of life will continue to be dominated by parental voices in our minds, some of which are supportive and others that are undermining.

At midlife, we can no longer afford to pretend that anyone other than ourselves is going to bring us the fulfillment we long for—not our spouse, lover, children, friends. Contrary to what actress Shirley MacLaine will tell you, this is our one and only life and it's up to us to make of it what we will. In my seminars, I ask women a question first posed by poet Mary Oliver: "What is it you want to do with this one wild and precious thing called your life?" It's a question that only you can answer.

What's Control Got to Do with It

Childhood is characterized by what psychoanalysts describe as "magical thinking"—the belief that we can control occurrences with our minds and that all our wishes are possible. Remember when you used to sing, "Rain, rain, go away. Come again another day"? Or when you thought the sun rose in the morning because you woke up and that it set in the evening because, like you, it was tired?

When my daughter was five or six, we used to play a game while we were stopped at a traffic light. We would sit at a red light and chant, "Light turn green; light turn green." When I saw that the light was about to change, I would say, "Blow," and she would blow and, sure enough, the light would change. That was power—that was a sense of control.

For a time, children need that innocent vision of living where everything happens for a reason and they have power, control, and significance. Without this illusion, they would be overwhelmed by a world that feels unpredictable and unmanageable. Even as adults, we want some reassurance, some sense of order—that we have control over the events in our lives. Novelist and essayist Albert Camus wrote, "A world that can be explained even with bad reason is a familiar world."

If we scratch the surface of our illusions, we find fear.

It's a fear rooted in childhood—a time when we weren't able to survive on our own. Our fear is of abandonment, rejection, and, ultimately, death. We carry our childhood beliefs into our adult lives to ward off the reality of how little power, control, and significance we actually have. As we saw with Allison, we usually sustain that pretense until life intervenes and makes us face our helplessness.

Most of us still cling to the belief that we're different—somehow set apart from the rest of humanity. We imagine that we have an exemption from the harshness of life. Bad things happen, but not to us; the truth, however, is that we aren't privileged. We will not be spared loss, failure, sorrow. We will not be protected from illness or death. Life doesn't distinguish between saints and sinners when it dishes out its share of tragedies and disasters. We're ordinary. What happens to other people also happens to us.

When the fantasy of our specialness crumbles, we're forced to see ourselves and the world in a radically different way. It's more difficult for us to pretend that we have it all together. We feel exposed. We're confronted with how little control we actually have and how little we know. Another layer of our illusions is peeled back. We become open to life—not as we thought it should be, but as it is. This is truly humbling.

Still, most of us build our lives in such a way as to stave off our anxiety about how little control we have. A friend of mine sent me a quote that I keep over my desk: "Our faith in our ability to control the future would be touching if it weren't so absurd. . . ." We cling to the pretense that we write the scripts for our lives. When we find ourselves in a difficult situation, when nothing seems to work, we try to manipulate life so that things will turn out the way we think they ought to. But more often than not, this just adds to our anxiety and despair.

Getting to Know Our Demons

"When you try to stay on the surface of the water, you sink; but when you try to sink, you float," writer Alan Watts said. "When you hold your breath you lose it. . . . Insecurity is the result of trying to be secure, and that contrariwise, salvation and sanity consist in the most radical recognition that we have no way of saving ourselves."

Most of us want to run from our fear. We want to be anyone but who we are and be anywhere but here. Gaining greater maturity involves getting to know our demons and the insecurity they evoke. Most of us consider anger, disappointment, resentment, and frustration as feelings we should avoid. Our emotions actually bring us information about the issues we're facing and what we need. If we accept that struggle and pain are an inherent part of life and are willing to learn from difficult situations, we can discover a new sense of freedom. Even when we have no idea of how things are going to turn out, if we allow ourselves to accept what's occurring, and acknowledge our feelings, no matter how painful they may be, the situation will become more manageable.

Each time we stand our ground and face our fear, it loses some of its power. Each time we meet a situation that we're certain we can't handle, that we feel is going to overwhelm us, and we get to the other side, we discover the enormity of our inner resources. One of the hallmarks of maturity is realizing that the outcome of any given sit-

uation is far less significant than how we cope with the
challenges we face. Do we run away, or hunker down for a
fight? Do fear and doubt overcome us? How can we begin
to work with our reactions?

We are now the rescuer, protector, caretaker. We are the
ones who tell ourselves the truth about what is occurring.
We can give ourselves the reassurance we desire, not
based on illusion, but on the reassurance of reality—of
what is. Then we can become familiar, even comfortable,
with the idea that life is change, and that we're never
going to get the proverbial ground under our feet, at least
not for more than just a minute.

The true test of spiritual growth is to learn to tolerate
uncertainty, to withstand the pain, disappointment, and
feelings of despair. As we do, we expand our awareness
and begin to discover how to navigate the ever-changing
seas of life. When we endure the insecurity, when we learn
to get comfortable in the middle of turmoil, when we remain steadfast as our emotions threaten to overwhelm us,
we experience a deepening—a stronger connection with
our essential self.

Ram Dass tells a story of a man who had a horse that ran
away. When his neighbor found out, he came over and
said, "That's terrible." The man said, "You never know."
The next day, the horse came back and was leading two
wild horses. The neighbor said, "That's wonderful." The
man said, "You never know." The man's only son was training one of the wild horses and fell off and broke his leg.
The neighbor came over and said, "That's terrible." The
man said, "You never know." The Cossack army came
through the village and recruited everyone. They took all
the young men. But they didn't take the son because he

had a broken leg. Again, the neighbor said, "That's wonderful." And again, the man said, "You never know." And it goes on and on. That is how life is; we make all kinds of assumptions. But the truth is, we don't really know anything.

Most of us assume that because a situation is painful, difficult, or unpleasant, that it's bad. It is often an unforeseen blessing. Each time things fall apart, life is teaching us about impermanence. Notice your reaction. When we lose our footing, it's another opportunity to strengthen our connection with ourselves and to take yet another step into the unknown. At midlife, we must learn to live with a greater degree of uncertainty and humility. In admitting how little we truly know, we gain wisdom. What we're really talking about is growing up.

Growing up means we abandon our simplified view of life and integrate its paradoxes. It means learning to tolerate ambiguities. It means being honest with ourselves and recognizing our limitations. Growing up means accepting that our longing for perfect safety and unconditional love will never be achieved. It means assuming responsibility for our own care, protection, and fulfillment. It means appreciating our uniqueness and inherent value. Growing up means setting attainable goals for ourselves, making compromises, and inserting realistic expectations in the place of our youthful grandiosity. It means being compassionate with ourselves.

At the time of our last session, Allison and I had scheduled a follow-up meeting. When she walked into my office, she looked older, although it had only been three months since I had last seen her. There was a solidity and confidence that I had not seen earlier. She told me that she had half a dozen clients and was getting inquiries daily. Her new career was well under way. "My practice is going really well and I'm thrilled," she said. "But I think I'm far more realistic as a result of my recent experiences. I was shocked that everything hadn't come to me the way I expected it to and that life wasn't going to be all that I ever dreamt it would be. It really hit me that I'm not omnipotent. I'm not this person who can do anything and everything. It was a real shock.

"But there's something wonderful about coming to terms with that, too," she continued. "It's made me scale down my expectations and invest myself in what's right in front of me. I have more of an attitude of Okay, this is what I have to work with, so I better throw myself into it and make the most magnificent life for myself that I can. It's been strangely comforting to come to terms with my limitations. I feel relieved."

At midlife, we become disillusioned, not in the sense of becoming cynical, but in beginning to see life more clearly. The definition of disillusionment is to expose falsehood, to open one's eyes, to accept reality. As we break the spell of our childhood illusions, we experience a greater sense of reality. This allows us to evaluate ourselves and the world more accurately.

If we haven't already become a famous rock star, neuro-surgeon, or CEO of a Fortune 500 company, it's probably not going to happen. Maybe that's really all right. Maybe life is less about what we achieve and more about how we live moment to moment, day to day.

A Lesson in Surrender

At the end of my daughter's senior year in high school, we decided to take a trip to the island in British Columbia where she was born. Neither of us had been back since she, her father, and I had left some sixteen years earlier.

Shortly after we arrived, we visited an old friend who's a jeweler. When she noticed me admiring one of her chrysanthemum rocks, she offered to make me a piece of jewelry if I found the right stone while on the island.

From that moment on, I was on a quest. Every time I went for a walk, I would scour the beach. I must have picked up several hundred stones. After days of intensive hunting, I began to notice that I had become obsessed with finding "the perfect rock." Without having realized it, I had gotten to the point where I was no longer enjoying myself. In fact, I was making myself miserable. Here I was in this idyllic setting, but I felt as stressed-out as I had been in Los Angeles. I had become so driven to find a keepsake of our trip that I was missing the actual experience. I called off my search, and for the first time since arriving, I began to feel like I was on vacation.

A few days later, I ran into an old friend, who invited me to go on a picnic. We rode our bikes to a deserted beach. As we lay on our stomachs at the water's edge, I suddenly noticed something tickling my palm. I looked down and there was a jet black stone with a perfectly formed circle etched on its oval surface. The stone was exactly the right size for my ring finger. I was speechless. I had let go, given up, and yet, having expended no effort, I had found the very thing I had been looking for.

I began to think about how fear had driven much of my life. My self-assured veneer had camouflaged how truly frightened I had been—frightened that if I didn't push, nothing would happen. Perhaps, after this experience, I could begin to loosen my grip and allow myself to be carried more by life. Perhaps it was time to get my ego out of the way and allow something deeper to motivate me. Perhaps it was less about "making it happen" than it was about allowing myself to be guided by a deeper voice—a voice that had always existed, but one to which I had only intermittently listened. Perhaps it was time to allow the wisdom of my authentic self to be more present in my life—to heed the truth that I knew to be correct but had too often ignored.

After that experience, I began to practice trusting whenever, wherever, however I found an opportunity. Each time we choose to trust—and it's not always easy— our faith grows incrementally stronger. On those occasions when I feel fear rising in the pit of my stomach, I glance down at my ring as a concrete reminder of what's possible for each of us when we open ourselves and surrender.

Chapter 7

GHOSTS IN THE DARKNESS

Perhaps all the dragons of our lives are princesses who are only waiting to see us once beautiful and brave. Perhaps everything terrible is in its deepest being something helpless that wants help from us.

—RAINER MARIA RILKE

So you say you've been a "good girl" all your life—devoted wife, caring mother, responsible career woman, dutiful daughter. Well, I have news for you. Behind the facade of the kind, generous, loving, selfless, innocent girl lies a treasure trove of untapped wealth—a resource most of you don't even know exists. But as is true of acquiring any treasure, there's a price. In this case, the price is leaving the world of the girl you'd like to think you are and recognizing your "bad girl." Come on now, don't pretend you don't know her. She's the angry, competitive, insecure, jealous, ambitious, selfish one—the aspects of your personality you've long kept hidden, even from yourself.

Throughout our lives, we've banished unwanted aspects of our personality into what psychoanalyst Carl Jung described as "our shadow." Poet Robert Bly calls it "the long bag we drag behind us." Accordingly, that bag contains all the characteristics that were disapproved of by the people we counted on for our survival. As you might imagine, by midlife our bags have become pretty darn full and all those suppressed parts are clamoring to get out: Like a group of women who have just returned from a silent retreat, everyone has plenty to say.

As young adults, many of us survived by figuring out how to adapt to the expectations of our parents, teachers, lovers, clergy, bosses, children. A good deal of our focus was on pleasing others and proving ourselves. We constructed a false self to satisfy or impress others. But at midlife, the effort to sustain that false self is draining and self-defeating. If a woman chooses not to reclaim the abandoned parts of herself, she becomes stuck, rigid, superficial. She'll go through the motions without the depth and richness of really living.

One of the primary tasks of midlife is to move beyond our limited view of ourselves. With the new awareness of our own mortality, we're no longer willing to deny the qualities and dreams we neglected during the first half of our lives. We want to bring our personality into greater balance. The call now is for us to be authentically ourselves. Whatever has been unlived must be integrated; whatever has been denied must be recognized; whatever has been silenced must be heard.

With many of the external structures—family, relationships, career—firmly in place, we can now turn our attention inward and ask ourselves, Who am I really? Many women awaken at midlife to the realization that they don't really know themselves as well as they thought. In fact, we're often surprised to discover that we have become black-and-white renditions of ourselves. This is no longer tolerable. The drive now is toward wholeness—to become the 3-D Technicolor women we truly are, to reclaim our unlived lives—our forgotten dreams, neglected qualities, and lost talents.

The concept of the shadow has been widely popularized in recent years. What I'd like to focus on is the importance of the integration of the lost self at midlife. While few women like to admit, even to themselves, that they're sometimes jealous, greedy, angry, and opportunistic, these qualities can bring a richness into our lives when they are acknowledged. By looking into the face of the shadow, by conceding that she's not always nice or as accommodating as a girl should be, a woman casts off her guise of innocence. Once she stops presenting herself as an ingenue, a woman creates a path for the second half of her life that permits complexity and depth.

Me and My Shadow

As young children, we were vital and energetic. But very quickly, many of us made unspoken agreements with teachers and the other significant adults in our lives to conceal the unacceptable aspects of ourselves. When we heard things like "Nice girls don't hit their brothers," or "Stop jumping around and act like a lady," or "Don't be smarter than the boys," or "Stop that whimpering or I'll really give you something to cry about," or "You better not win that game with Billy or he'll feel bad," or "Don't touch yourself," we cast into darkness all that was unacceptable. When a girl enters adolescence, society comes along with its pruning shears and further trims back other qualities that are considered "unfeminine."

As I discussed earlier in the book, Carol Gilligan describes how adolescent girls feel pressured by society to split into authentic and false selves. The social pressure is to show only those qualities and talents that are considered "feminine," pleasing, attractive. We learned how to present ourselves in a way that was, by and large, innocuous in order to earn approval, love, and protection. We learned to construct a false self. Simultaneously, then, a girl's ego—the outer presentation of self—and her shadow were created. Our shadow was constructed to protect us from rejection and abandonment. Here's an incident that occurred that made a major contribution to the development of my shadow.

I was nine years old and in third grade. My teacher's name was Miss Aires. She was what my mother called "a strict teacher." There was nothing fun about our third-grade class—Miss Aires was all business. I dreaded going to school—in part, because I had a lisp. At the time, my name was Thephanie Thmall. So I did everything possible not to talk during class. But Miss Aires had a different idea about how to cure me of what she thought was "an attention-getting device." Go figure.

We were studying Abraham Lincoln and for homework we were supposed to memorize the Gettysburg Address. I knew it by heart. The next morning, Miss Aires asked for a volunteer to come to the front of the class and recite it. I cowered at my desk, praying she wouldn't call on me. But no such luck.

I took a deep breath and prepared for disaster. I began, "Four thcore and theven yearth ago." I got no further before first one and then another kid began to giggle, until it seemed as if I had just told some hilarious joke. I looked down at the floor, trying to contain my tears, but I burst out crying. Miss Aires sternly commanded the class to be quiet, then told me to "stop the theatrics and finish." But I couldn't get another word out. Miss Aires accused me of not having done my homework. She asked who else would like to present Lincoln's speech?

I was instructed to return to my seat. As I walked back to my desk, I said under my breath, "I did too do my homework." Miss Aires heard me and asked if I had something more to say. I turned around and told her that I thought she was mean and that she wasn't fair.

She marched me out of the classroom, down the long tiled hallway, and into the office. I could hear her talking to the principal. After what felt like an hour, but which I'm sure was only a few minutes, Miss Aires left. The principal called me in and reprimanded me. I never did get to tell my side of the story. As a punishment, I had to stay in during recess and write one hundred times "I will not talk back to my teacher." As I sat alone in the classroom, I could hear the other kids outside on the playground.

That night at dinner when my parents asked me about school, I told them what had happened. My mother immediately took Miss Aires's side and scolded me for not being prepared and talking back to an adult. For the next several years, until my lisp disappeared, I tried to stay out of sight. I never volunteered to answer a question, though I often knew the answers. I decided that it wasn't worth the risk of humiliation.

What that experience taught me was that you must never allow yourself to be vulnerable for any reason. My vulnerability was banished into my shadow. Miss Aires, the principal, and my parents showed me that you should never challenge authority; when you do, you're shamed and punished. Bravery and fearlessness were stuffed into my shadow. When I told my parents of my plight and they turned against me, I learned that it wasn't safe to trust anyone. My ability to trust, which had already become an issue, was shoved into the shadow. Up until third grade, I had enjoyed school, but from this and similar experiences, I lost interest and felt defeated. There went my enthusiasm and self-confidence. This experience was emblematic of many other situations that not only changed my attitude about school but, more essentially, changed my sense of myself.

I'm sure you can recall incidents in your own life in which you felt disapproval and shame. Most of us have a bag choked full of them. While all of us have a personal bag that we drag around behind us, as women of the baby-boom generation we also share a collective shadow. The necessity to deny certain parts of ourselves is not solely psychological; it also occurs because of what society imposes on us. Despite the fact that many of us questioned the conventional values of the 1950s and early 1960s and were encouraged to go beyond "traditional feminine roles," countless women were still reluctant to permit themselves to throw off these constraints. Many of us were taught to "be nice," "be selfless," "be pretty," "be loving," "be supportive"—you get the idea. Even when we were encouraged to be smart and pursue an education and career, as well as husbands, these prefeminist values often linger and cloud our ability to express ourselves fully. While younger boomer women feel a greater degree of freedom, more often than we'd like to admit, our certainty, competitiveness, independence—anything that we thought might threaten our attractiveness—were often stuffed into the bag. For many of us who wanted to break the mold, we assumed male values and stashed away our vulnerability, neediness, intuition, insecurity. Either way, we lost precious parts of ourselves.

Unfortunately, many of the women I see in therapy have only a vague remembrance of the loss of their true self. They often feel a gnawing frustration about whether to allow others' opinions to define them or to express their own buried needs and feelings. Often, it's not until women reach midlife that they begin to uncover just how much of themselves they have banished.

Excuse Me, but Your Shadow's Showing

At midlife, our repressed parts often erupt. We find ourselves acting uncharacteristically. We don't feel like ourselves. As authors Connie Zweig and Stephen Wolf point out in their book *Romancing the Shadow*, the shadow appears in unexpected ways. An ordinarily devoted wife finds herself involved in a torrid affair. A caring, soft-spoken mother verbally attacks her child. A responsible hardworking woman, who has spent a great deal of energy developing her career, suddenly loses interest. The usually active woman, who works out regularly and watches her diet,

abandons her fitness regimen and sneaks down to the
kitchen in the middle of the night and finishes her son's
leftover pizza. The ever-appropriate socialite gets caught
with her shadow showing when she unexpectedly tells an
off-color joke at a dinner party. When these kinds of things
happen, we feel like we've been snatched by aliens. We
say things like "I can't believe I did that." Or "It's so unlike me." Or "I just wasn't myself." But you were yourself.
Just not the self you recognize. Another side of your personality has broken through and disrupted your well-
ordered life. At midlife, we often feel like a stranger to
ourselves. For many of us, it's a blessing in disguise. In the
Gospel of Thomas, it is said, "If you bring forth what is
within you, what you bring forth will save you. If you do
not bring forth what is within you, what you do not bring
forth will destroy you." I found that to be pretty good in-
centive to get to know my dark side. How about you? The
dark side demands to be incorporated into our lives. But
how do we recognize our shadow? Especially since, by definition, it is unconscious and can't be known directly.

Jung believed that what we were unwilling to face in
ourselves, we would be forced to encounter in the world.
We've all had the experience where we overreacted to a
quality or a certain behavior in someone else. We find that
person disgusting, unethical, reprehensible. Well, if you
haven't figured this out already, let me be the first to in-
form you that what you can't tolerate or acknowledge in
yourself, you often project onto others. In other words,
those qualities that we don't want to see in ourselves, we
tend to find in others. Let me give you an example.

I was having lunch with a friend recently, when she looked
across the room and saw a woman who worked in her law

firm. For the next several minutes, she ranted and raved about this woman. "You won't believe what she'll do to get ahead. It's embarrassing. Last week, she volunteered to go into work on the weekend to help one of the partners prepare a brief. It's pathetic. She's determined to have more billable hours than any of the rest of us. As my mother would say, 'She looks like a woman but acts like a man.' It's clear she's angling to make partner." It was obvious from my friend's reaction that this woman represented something that she was denying in herself. I knew that she had worked hard and had struggled over the years to get promoted. It had been obvious to me that she wanted more power and prestige, although she never would have admitted it. But she didn't recognize this in herself. In fact, she fancied herself to be rather laid-back, when, in fact, she was driven.

Spanish poet Antonio Machado illuminated the psychological idea of projection when he wrote, "Look for your other half, who walks next to you, and tends to be who you aren't." The quickest way to recognize your shadow is to ask yourself of whom are you most critical. Think about someone whom you dislike, someone who in your opinion possesses completely offensive qualities. On the other hand, whom do you idealize? You'll be surprised to know that whatever qualities you despise or envy in another are the aspects of your personality that you've rejected.

What we find intolerable in others lives within us. I know that it's pretty humbling to have to admit that we have our very own version of Mata Hari, Leona Helmsley, Cruella de Vil, Marilyn Monroe, Lorena Bobbit, Eva Braun, or Joan Crawford living inside us. While our shadows may not be as extreme as these individuals, trust me, they're there.

While we think of the shadow as primarily containing negative qualities, it also includes characteristics such as spontaneity, creativity, power, exuberance, sexuality— treasures locked away but just waiting to be reclaimed. As Jung so brilliantly reminds us, "We do not become enlightened by imagining figures of light, but by making the darkness conscious."

The Virtues of Being a Bad Girl

Bad girls don't hesitate to speak their minds and stand up for what they believe in. Bad girls don't walk on eggshells, and if they do, they wear stiletto heels. Bad girls aren't afraid to play hardball when it comes to negotiating a deal. Bad girls sometimes eat the last cookie without a second thought. Bad girls don't mind being called a bitch when the other person sits up and takes notice. Bad girls don't hesitate to fly to Los Angeles on the spur of the moment to catch a Springsteen concert. Bad girls have been known to settle in with a big bowl of warm chocolate pudding, their favorite video, unplug the phone, and disappear for the night. Bad girls throw caution to the wind and paint their house teal blue with lavender trim when every other house in the neighborhood is tastefully beige. Bad girls don't hesitate to take an occasional "mental health day" and go to a day spa for pampering. Bad girls say no without a moment's hesitation. Bad girls aren't afraid to dance with reckless abandon at a club that's filled with Gen Xers. Bad girls ask for what they want, and they may even have their request emblazoned in skywriting if that's what it takes to make their point. Bad girls aren't afraid to be seen in a sexy black dress cut up to there or down to *there*. Bad girls call in sick from time to time in order to stay home and make wild love with their partner. Bad girls are "age flashers"—they're middle-aged and proud of it. Bad girls have been known to leave a work-related seminar early and go to back-to-back matinees. Bad girls aren't afraid to teach their husbands how to operate heavy equipment like the washer and dryer. You get the point.

When I say *bad*, I mean it in the very best sense of the word. You know, bad, as in being boldly, unabashedly yourself. There's something truly freeing about throwing off the personal and societal constraints and allowing yourself to be fully who you are, rather than the edited, sanitized version you've lived with most of your life. I don't know about you, but I don't trust anyone who's too nice or too good. You know that what you're seeing is just the tip of the iceberg. And as we all know, when it comes to icebergs, it's what's below the surface that causes disasters.

At midlife, the shadow blows holes in our good-girl persona. We're being asked to restructure our entire personality around a new center—our authentic self. We're being called to expand our identity—to incorporate our dark side so that a larger, truer self can come forth. I don't know about you, but I find that there's something deliciously exciting about the idea of having a dark side—a side of yourself that you know contains a warehouse full of forbidden fruits. But most of us have shied away from exploring this part of our personality for fear that it would sweep us away—that we'd go wild and wouldn't be able to maintain our nice-girl image.

But when we finally realize that no matter how good we are, no matter how well behaved, no one is going to protect us or keep us safe, then we can explore our shadow. The untapped qualities and abandoned dreams that reside there are like embers smoldering in the ashes, just waiting for us to fan them into a flame that will revitalize our lives.

Olly Olly Oxen Free: It's Safe to Come Home Now

Like many of us, Jean felt the need to write a new, more inclusive story for the second half of her life. A fifty-two-year-old epidemiologist, she had grown up the eldest of five children in a strict, religious family in a small rural farming community. Her family worked hard just to keep food on the table. For as long as she could remember, every day both before and after school there were chores to be done. As a child, Jean loved to dance. But whenever her mother saw her, she forbade Jean to "waste her time on such foolishness." As she talked to me about her childhood, she broke down. "I had to sneak and hide in my room in order to do anything fun. It felt like a sin." She pulled herself together and continued. "I should be over this by now. That was another lifetime ago. But it still haunts me. My life was and to some extent still is so serious. Sometimes I feel like I'm going to explode."

Jean was the only person in her family to go to college. She would have loved to have studied dance, but that was never an option. She had to do something practical. Consequently, she spent years building her career. But in the past month, she had found herself bored with her work and not wanting to go to the lab. I suspected that unlived parts of her personality were beginning to stir.

When I mentioned this, Jean told me of a recent incident with her nephew that had alarmed her. He and her sister were visiting one Sunday, and he wanted to play a game with her. Jean was in the middle of writing a report. "I just lashed out at him. I sounded just like my mother. It startled me." As we explored her reaction, Jean realized that her nephew was calling on her to be playful and spontaneous, two qualities she had locked away years ago. Yet these were aspects of her life she was now longing for. The more we talked about her playfulness, the more uneasy she became. She had abandoned her creative side in order to be practical. Jean didn't know how to find a balance in her life that would allow her to inhabit both worlds.

I asked what came to mind when she thought about letting herself play. Her initial reaction was reluctance. "I feel like if I let myself do something fun, I'll be like the Energizer bunny and just keep going. When I finally let myself play with my nephew, I felt a bit sad. I realized how much of myself I'd given up. But it also scared me. I felt like if I let myself go, I could just run wild." Over the next several weeks, we explored her fears. These feelings were unfamiliar and, consequently, threatening. I reassured Jean that it was highly unlikely that she would run off and join the circus or a dance company. But her concern was what might happen after having kept herself on such a tight rein for so many years.

When we become aware of our shadow, we have an opportunity to reclaim it. When we acknowledge our unwanted parts, they often become more manageable. After addressing her fears, I suggested that Jean either go out dancing or sign up for a dance class. That was the beginning of a significant change. After a couple of months, she not only decided to do jazz dance but she also added a samba class. "I can't believe how much fun I'm having. I almost don't recognize myself." Much to her delight, Jean was not only experiencing pleasure and playfulness but she discovered a renewed vitality and increased energy for her work.

It's not that we should give in to all of our long-denied needs and dreams and throw away those things that we've worked so hard to build. But we can't afford to ignore our unlived life, either. We must learn to balance our competing needs. Jean was an "all work and no play" kind of girl. By incorporating some of the neglected aspects of her personality into her everyday life, she was able to discover a greater sense of wholeness and was on the path to leading a fuller life.

As writer Carolyn McKensie suggests, "If you have a skeleton in your closet, take it out and dance with it." The shadow forces us to express ourselves in new ways. We have to acknowledge the parts of us that have been ignored, and respect and honor what they're trying to tell us.

Xena, Warrior Princess: Reclaiming Our Power

If the goal of our mothers' generation was to marry a stable man who would be a good provider, it's no wonder that power, anger, and aggression were banished from our lives. They threatened the very essence of all that our mothers considered precious. Can you imagine Donna Reed complaining to her husband that she was sick and tired of cooking dinner every night or June telling Ward that she thought she was wasting her talents and was going to start a career? It would never have happened. The majority of women just didn't do those sorts of things.

Our mothers aspired to be models of femininity, and they wanted their daughters to be the same—sweet, docile, pleasing, pretty girls. There was no room in this picture for a woman to be powerful. Remember the old nursery rhyme—"Sugar and spice and everything nice; That's what little girls are made of"? Well, the truth is, girls were supposed to go heavy on the sugar and hold the spice. We all knew that men don't like uppity women. The ideal woman was one who was compliant and helpless. As long as she remained in this state, she could borrow power from a man. After all, it was considered taboo for her to have any power of her own.

Yet despite the fact that women have had to deny their strength and authority, our feelings of anger are inextricably tied with our sense of authority. Our anger can motivate and mobilize us to take action, to speak out on our own behalf, to stand up for what we think and believe. While we all know that venting rage is ineffective and off-putting, anger expressed appropriately is a way to clarify and assert our thoughts, feelings, and needs. It awakens our healthy protectiveness and strength. It's a way for us to recover ourselves.

There's tremendous power in the word *no*. But we usually have to reach our limit before we're willing to say it. It's only by saying no to one thing that we make room for something else. When we say, "No, I will not remain in the background any longer" or "No, you can't treat me this way," we inevitably create change. In a broader sense, it was the women of the suffrage movement saying, "No, we will no longer remain the property of men" that eventually won us the right to vote. It was a woman saying, "No, I will not ride in the back of the bus" that fanned the flames of the civil rights movement. It was women saying, "No, I will not allow you to send our sons to war" and supporting them in resisting the draft during the Vietnam War. It is women who now say, "No, I will not allow you to dictate what I can and cannot do with my body when it comes to reproductive rights." Imagine what would happen if women stood together and collectively said no to all the injustice in the world. You can be certain that things would change.

We all know that women have been pissed off forever. And with good reason. Society has marginalized and mistreated women for centuries. Women were seen as second-class citizens—the "second sex." I don't know about you, but I get riled up just thinking about it. But let's face it, who wants to walk around with a scarlet *B* branded on her chest. People, especially people of the male persuasion, don't like it when a woman gets angry or asserts herself. Admit it, how many times have you heard a man walk around singing the Cat Stevens lyric "I'm looking for a hard headed woman"? How about never. So it's no wonder that anger, the source of much of our power, went underground. Who would want to be sentenced to a life as a shrew, a witch, a ball-buster, or a nag? Not any woman I know.

Until the sixties, aggression and anger were largely disowned by women in our society. While our culture supported women's quest for equality, we were expected to put everyone else's needs before our own. And, above all, we were never supposed to utter a discouraging word. Even women who pursued careers were expected to be hopelessly devoted to their husbands and family, ever cheerful, adaptable, understanding. But that was the ideal, the model women were supposed to strive for. I don't know about you, but I'd rather shoot myself.

Since women were expected to be peacekeepers, it's often difficult for us to assert our sense of power. This not only robbed us of much of our energy but also prevented us from recognizing the full extent of our strength and capability. Surprisingly, even women in positions of authority often feel uneasy when they're confronted with having to disrupt the status quo. Mary Beth is one such woman. A forty-six-year-old managing editor of a trade newspaper, she is attractive, with shoulder-length dark brown hair.

"When I was in my twenties, I had a choice between going to law school and going into the mines. I went to the coalfields," Mary Beth told me. "I felt like it was a calling. It was work that I really cared about. It was with people I really cared about." After ten years working underground, Mary Beth was offered a position with the mine workers' union doing labor organizing. She and her husband moved to Washington. As part of her job, she became active in the Network of Women Miners. But when she began to champion women's issues, she was suddenly fired.

Mary Beth decided to file a sex-discrimination suit against the union. "I was torn up inside," she said. "Underneath all my anger and hurt was a genuine love for the union. I felt emotionally loyal. So it was very hard for me to turn around and sue them." Not only did Mary Beth have a strong investment in the union but she also cherished the community of women miners. Like so many women, Mary Beth equated change with loss. And, in fact, she did have a great deal to lose. Yet despite what was at stake, she felt that she had to make others aware of the injustice that had occurred.

While her husband was supportive of her decision, her family was not. Both her mother and father told her that she was going to ruin her life. "I think I learned to be a people-pleaser growing up," she said. "That came from my father, whom I'm very much like in a lot of ways. We lived in a town where the John Birch Society was active. I can still remember my mother answering the phone and being on the verge of telling them to go to hell. My father would jump in and say to her, 'Well, well, well, we don't say that kind of thing, dear.' He would coach her, telling her to pretend that she was busy whenever they would call her to go to a meeting. His philosophy was to avoid conflict at all cost."

"Talk about conflict," I said to Mary Beth.

"No kidding," she replied. "Part of me knew I had to file the suit and another part was screaming at me not to make waves. But I had to. Even though I had no idea of what the outcome would be, I felt strongly that I had to do it." Despite the fact that Mary Beth risked the disapproval of family friends and coworkers, she'd gained her self-respect. She could no longer limit herself to being the person she thought she should be. She was stepping beyond the self she had constructed during the first half of her life to please her parents and society. The power and assertiveness she had rejected as a child were now clamoring to be reclaimed.

But there were times when Mary Beth felt nervous and afraid. She felt threatened. She didn't attend the Women Miners' conferences because she knew that many of the male union leaders would be in attendance and her case was the subject of a great deal of discussion. A friend was afraid that if she testified on Mary Beth's behalf, her trailer would be burned down. Her friend ultimately decided not to.

"I felt very isolated at times and uncertain," Mary Beth told me. "Many of my friends distanced themselves from

me. Aside from my husband, I felt pretty alone. But I discovered new resources in myself that I didn't know existed. I was scared to death to go to the deposition and I
was scared to go to court. But I found that during the de-
positions, I could be articulate and I could speak with
conviction. I knew that I had convictions. But it was when
I was under pressure that it really came out. I saw that I
could handle the barrage from the union attorneys. That
gave me a lot of strength." She had broken through the
confining patterns of having to play it safe. She was gaining a new sense of integrity. *Webster's* defines integrity as
"the quality or state of being complete, unbroken." Mary
Beth had arrived at a place in her life where she could
honor and approve of her choices and her own life.

Despite her growing confidence, Mary Beth was understandably concerned about having to appear in court. Several of the opposing counsel had been her friends. In
preparation for the trial, her attorney took her into the
empty courtroom. "I walked up to the witness chair and
just sat in it," she said. "And I knew that that was my
place. This was not a place where I was going to be a victim. This was a place of power. This was a place of truth.
Even though the legal system is not always about justice
and truth, it was for me. And I'm grateful for that. When
it was all over, I felt like a different person. I was no longer
innocent. I saw the world more clearly, and I was way more
confident." Although Mary Beth's decision to sue the
union was rooted in righting an injustice, the result was
that she integrated disparate parts of her personality and
felt more authentic, more whole. As is true for many of us,
when we survive a potentially destructive situation, we
are forever changed by the experience.

Mary Beth won the case against the union. Not only did she win in terms of her legal victory but she also won in terms of extending her sense of power into the larger world. "Since the case has been closed, my life now is about following my passion—whatever that proves to be. If you're going to live your life fully, it seems that you can't avoid conflict. Waves, no waves—life is filled with waves, and I've learned that it's okay to make them, and when I have to, I can ride them."

I'm Pissed, but in a Good Way!

Even if anger is tied to our power, what woman in her right mind would want to let her anger out of the bag? Yet for many midlife women, we just don't have much of a choice. Blame it on hormones. In fact, our testosterone level does increase during menopause, but never to the level that exists in men. Women often do experience a greater balance between their masculine and feminine nature. But that seems like only one facet of this complex picture. More importantly, the immense psychological changes we experience during midlife have caused our disowned power to burst forth.

Ellen, a fifty-three-year-old tall blond woman with classic features, had been married to Peter for twenty-two years. Ten years into their relationship, her husband had an affair. When Ellen found out, she was distraught, but she minimized the impact of the betrayal. She was terrified of losing her marriage and expressed more hurt than anger. But now, after another ten years, Ellen discovered a copy of a love letter Peter had sent to a woman who worked in his office.

When Ellen confronted Peter, he admitted he had been having an affair. Her immediate reaction was that she wanted a divorce. "I can't believe Peter did this," she said quietly. "I never thought that he'd do this again. I feel like such a fool." Ellen had ignored all the danger signs, of which there had been many.

It wasn't surprising, given the fact that she had grown up with an alcoholic mother and a stepfather, both of whom were extremely critical and demeaning. Ellen learned early not to make any demands and not to express any feelings other than happiness and contentment. As a result, she rarely asserted her needs or expressed her feelings.

After continuing to share a bedroom with her husband for several days, Ellen found it intolerable and moved into the guest room. At the end of a week of feeling displaced, the thought dawned on her, Why should I be inconvenienced? He's the one who should move. It was then that Ellen took the first in a number of uncharacteristic steps. She asked Peter to move out. His initial reaction was one of shock. "While I was with him, I couldn't afford to get angry. I was too dependent on him," she said. But over the next several months, Ellen began to discover a new self-protectiveness and strength, qualities that had been banished into her shadow years ago.

While anger is a frightening emotion, especially for women, it often motivates change. It challenges the status quo, ruffles feathers, and causes even the most powerful man to grow uneasy. But anger is an important messenger, one that shouldn't be ignored. In her groundbreaking book *The Dance of Anger*, Harriet Lerner points out that anger signals that we aren't getting our needs sufficiently fulfilled or that we're being hurt or ignored. Our anger lets us know that we have compromised or sacrificed too much of ourselves. It often helps us to question and define what it is we want and need for ourselves and in our own lives. In Ellen's case, her anger propelled her to take action on her own behalf. Although she felt uncomfortable expressing anger, it was essential that she do so. Like many women, Ellen had been conditioned by her family as well as by society to fear her anger and, consequently, her power. As women, we often worry that by expressing anger and asserting our needs, we will perhaps upset, even destroy our relationships. But paradoxically, it is often our silence that harms them.

Ellen talked about how no one had ever given her permission to defend herself. She admitted feeling awkward and unsure of this neglected side of her personality. The challenge for Ellen, as it is for many women, was to balance her vulnerability with her emerging sense of power.

Ellen came into my office one day and confessed, "I let Peter have it the other day. He'd called and started to tell me how he really wanted what was best for me. How he'd realized that we were fundamentally incompatible. And how he had found his soul mate. He tried to convince me that I didn't need to get an attorney. That we could work out a settlement ourselves, with his financial adviser. It took me a moment, but I cut him off and told him that I had already spoken with an attorney. When he started to argue with me, I just hung up. I hardly recognized myself."

For the first time in her life, Ellen was going to make sure that she would receive what was rightfully hers. She had begun to protect herself. By listening to her own feelings and desires, Ellen was beginning to regain neglected aspects of her personality. Like so many women, when

Ellen allowed herself to feel angry, she was taking a risk in order to gain a new freedom. An essential aspect of recovering our power is for women to speak out on their own behalf. Our passion and energy is tied to our anger. I firmly believe that a woman who is pissed off has enough energy to electrify a small country.

Beyond Inhibition

Another aspect of reclaiming our power at midlife is recognizing our capability and strength. Many of the women I interviewed were just now realizing how competent they were, despite years of having been successful in careers and running households. During the first half of their lives, many women often played it safe. But at midlife, women find that they're more willing to undertake projects in which they are forced to move beyond what's familiar. In some cases, it's simply for the challenge. But more often than not, it's born of a desire to support a cause they believe in passionately. As a result, they discover previously unknown abilities.

It had been five years since Lisa, a fifty-six-year-old visual artist, had been diagnosed and successfully treated for breast cancer. She was working on a series of puti, Italian cherubs, when a nurse from the cancer center contacted her. She had had an idea for raising money for breast cancer research. The nurse asked if Lisa would design an angel that could be made into an ornament and sold. "We had no idea of what we were doing," Lisa said. "All I knew was that I wanted to do something to help the cause, and making a piece of art was right up my alley." But that was just the beginning. When they had a finished product, the hard work of finding a manufacturer who would produce the sculptures, networking, and fund-raising lay ahead.

"Creating the angel was wonderful," Lisa said, "but going forward with all the business stuff, I was really outside my comfort zone." I asked Lisa what made it so difficult. "It was hard for me to ask people for something. It just wasn't something I could do. My father died when I was four. Although we were well taken care of financially, my mother had made it blatantly clear that you just shouldn't ask for anything. Looking back on it, I just don't think she had anything to give. That message has stuck with me all these years. I'd never worked in volunteer organizations raising money, doing any of that. I just couldn't put myself in a position to have to ask someone for help. But something came over me." I asked Lisa what was different. "I had put so much into the design of our angel that I simply wasn't willing to lose everything I'd worked for. Besides, I really believed in what we were doing. I guess necessity really is the mother of empowerment. An artist friend sent me a little statuette of Xena. You know, the Warrior Princess. She'd had a makeover. Along with her standard-issue sword and shield, she now had salt-and-pepper hair and was wearing a diaphanous skirt and cape. I've named her 'my menopausal action figure.' I keep her on my desk. Every time I had to make a call or do something that was a stretch, I'd look at her and gather my strength." Lisa sent letters to the three major manufacturers of ornaments. She and her partner attained non-profit status for their project.

"I was in my studio painting away, and within a week I got calls from the CEOs of all three companies," she continued.

"I was stunned and thrilled. When they called back, I suddenly felt I did have some capability. I could do this." A year later, she and her partner made their first donation to UCLA's Jonsson Comprehensive Cancer Center. "We now have a Web site and are going to be in a number of the national department stores. It's really just been a grassroots thing. This has been an amazing learning experience for me about myself and about what can happen when you're willing to ask for things. It just brings out the best in people really. People do want to help. I saw that I could really do some things. It opened the door to no boundaries anymore."

During midlife, women begin to realize that they can achieve whatever they set their sights on. Well, maybe not everything. We're probably not going to set any track records (at least for women under forty!) or suddenly become the most famous opera star in the world. But this is exactly the moment when we should challenge ourselves to achieve the things we thought we couldn't do. This is one of the great, inspiring things about this period. Who cares if you're not going to win the world figure-skating championship, if you discover that you can, in fact, skate and you love it? What does it matter if your watercolors will never be seen by the masses or your rose garden isn't going to appear in Martha Stewart *Living*, if you find pleasure and satisfaction in a new creative expression?

At midlife, we must remember our power. But our sense of power is not the same kind as what we've seen abused throughout history. Most women don't want to have anything to do with power that manipulates, controls, and is lorded over another person. What most women want is a feminine power—a power that recognizes our interdependence and interconnectedness, that respects and honors differences. As writer Carolyn Heilbrun says, "Power is the ability to take one's place in whatever discourse is essential to action and the right to have one's part matter."

We can no longer pretend to be weak. We can no longer pretend to be innocent. We can no longer pretend to be a victim. As women face their fears about asserting themselves, they begin to recognize how far they've come. They begin to realize what's possible when they are willing to act in their own best interest and take a stand for what they value.

Telling It Like It Is

Since childhood, women have been taught to mistrust their own experiences and to keep their mouths shut. I'm kind of appalled when I think back on it. But on my bedroom wall, I had a plaque that showed three monkeys, one covering its eyes, another its ears, and the third its mouth. What was I thinking? It's obvious now that I wasn't thinking. But this sentiment seems to have been a motto of girls who grew up in the late forties and fifties. We were conditioned not to see what we see, hear what we hear, or speak what we know. Girls were taught not to raise difficult issues.

One of the essential goals of midlife is learning to trust our deepest nature and to give it voice. This requires that we haul our honesty and directness out of that dusty old bag we've been dragging around and become the outspoken, rabble-rousing firebrand who was once banished. I'm not suggesting that we return to the days when our forcefulness often manifested itself as stridency and intolerance, but, rather, that we become passionately protective of our own rights as well as those of others.

During midlife, as we integrate our disowned power, it becomes easier to take charge with a ferocity that has been tempered by time. I had an experience in which I wasn't able to keep my pantherlike self under wraps. I'd gone to the dentist to get my teeth cleaned. As the hygienist put the napkin around my neck, I noticed that she was coughing and sneezing. I asked if she was sick. She said, "I have a cold, but I'm almost over it."

"Are you still contagious?" I asked somewhat reluctantly.

She replied, "No, I'm not that sick."

I tried to settle down. But I couldn't ignore my growing discomfort.

"Do you think you should be working?" I asked.

"I can't miss work just for a cold," she shot back.

As I sat in the chair, I had visions of her germs engulfing me for the hour that she was going to be working in my mouth. What's more, I was leaving the next day to go away for Thanksgiving.

I finally burst out, "I'm not comfortable."

"It's no worse than if you went to the grocery store," she said. Without thinking, I got up from the chair, put on my jacket, and said, "I'll come back another time." I rescheduled my appointment. In years past, I might have politely nailed myself to the chair, but no longer. For what?

One of our responsibilities as we emerge from this passage is that we speak the truth, the truth about what we have learned, the truth about what we see, the truth that lives in our hearts. We now have the responsibility to speak because we are the ones who know.

Embracing Our Wholeness

As we begin to acknowledge that there's more to us than what we reveal in our everyday lives, we invite in all of our humanness. Imagine how much energy is tied up in our need to repress what we have long considered unacceptable—all the passion, creativity, intellectual and sexual energy just waiting to be released. There's gold in our shadow, but in order to tap into this resource, we must accept ourselves in our full measure, our vices along with our virtues. For every quality we embody, we also hold the opposite. Anyone who is generous, for example, is also greedy. Anyone who's strong is also insecure. Indeed, every woman embodies a range of emotions, some complementary, some contradictory.

One of the tasks of this passage is to appreciate complexity and to tolerate ambiguity. Midlife is when we can embrace our limitations, along with our strengths. As we accept our anger, insecurity, envy, resentment, neediness—those aspects of our personalities we've long kept hidden—we can see ourselves more clearly not for the person we hoped we would be but for who we are, and in this way, we can become comfortable in our own skin.

Chapter 8

WE ALL NEED SOMEBODY TO LEAN ON

A friend is someone you can call in the middle of the night when your man is gone, or you wish he would go, or you suspect your cellulite is winning—or even just to prove to yourself that there is someone you can call in the middle of the night.

—ANNE BEATTS

My women friends are lifesavers. I don't know what I'd do without them." "They're my soul sisters. They are always there when I need them." "My female friends steady me. I can tell them anything."

These are some of the many comments made by the women I interviewed. Whether married, never married, divorced, or widowed, every woman I spoke with talked about the essential role friendships with other women played in their lives. When we're in the midst of intense self-examination, we often rely on our women friends in a similar way as we did when we were teenagers. When we're undergoing such a significant transformation, we naturally seek the company of other women, and most particularly women our own age, perhaps because we're facing similar issues and challenges—our bodies are changing; our sense of ourselves is changing; people close to us have become ill or died. By sharing our struggles and experiences, we find comfort—we feel less alone. For all of these reasons and more, our women friends become more central at midlife.

It's not that we don't like men; quite the contrary, in fact. But you have to admit, they're different creatures. Let's face it, how many men jump at the opportunity to spend an hour talking about their intimate thoughts and feelings? Men tend to focus on problem solving. They often take the fix-it approach to life. They're more comfortable discussing practical matters and ideas. There's a level of emotional intimacy and equality that women experience with women that rarely exists with a man. We love to ramble aimlessly through our internal landscape—no agenda, no planned outcome—just to listen and be listened to.

Only another woman can commiserate about being awakened out of a deep sleep by the sudden surge of heat scorching our bodies or feeling as if we've misplaced our minds along with our keys. Only another woman can laugh about having to travel with a separate suitcase for our nutritional supplements or celebrate that we no longer have to worry about getting pregnant. Only another woman can understand our horror at discovering that we have crepe-paper thighs and no longer fit into our favorite gabardine slacks. As we go through this momentous passage, we need the camaraderie of other women.

We Are Family—I Got All My Sisters with Me

As our parents age and die, as our children scatter across the country, and as our marriages end or change, our friendships with other women become more precious to us and take on greater importance. Several women described their friends as becoming "their chosen family," or said, "She's more my sister than my blood sister" or "She's the sister of my heart."

Paula, a fifty-one-year-old divorced mother with grown children, echoed this sentiment: "My friends are my support system, my life line, my reality check. I don't think I could get through the day without my friends. Like it or not, they're in my life forever." This sentiment was expressed by many of the women I interviewed, both married and single. "Andy is my lover, my sweetheart, my mate," said Carolyn, a fifty-two-year-old woman who has been married to her second husband for fifteen years. "But when something comes up where I need to feel listened to, I call my women friends. They're just right there. They understand me in a way I don't think a man can."

Many women are often more comfortable sharing the intricacies of their emotional lives with friends rather than with family members. As our parents age, we're less willing to burden them with our concerns. But also, there's often a greater sense of safety and support among our women friends. Many of the women I spoke with didn't feel that their families understood them as they are now. They felt as if their families had frozen them in a role they had been cast in during childhood. It was as if their biological families didn't see them as the changing, maturing women they are.

We often discover that our friends are more willing to recognize our maturing selves, that the love and acceptance we've wanted from our families is often more available from our women friends. "When my mother died three years ago, I realized the necessity of creating a family of my heart," said Lorna, a forty-nine-year-old vice president of a bank. "I chose women whom I could be myself with. You can't always be that with your family. Whom do I want to spend the rest of my life with? I'm picking people who are going on the boat with me. At midlife, there's a sense of taking hold of my life in all sorts of ways. One way is to say, 'These women are my family and I want to deepen my connection with them. I'm going to know this person forever and I'm committing to that.'"

Within the safety of a trusted friendship, we can explore our fears, our dreams—our private selves. Our female friends provide clarity and understanding. They encourage in each of us the woman we are becoming.

You've Gotta Have Friends

"My husband almost embodies a good female friend," Felicia, a fifty-year-old museum curator, said. "It's one of the miracles of our relationship. But there are differences for sure. With him, I'm somewhat guarded. Much less so than with any other man, but it's still there. I don't tell him everything that I'd tell one of my women friends. I have to be careful what I tell him about my mother or my children, because he's part of the whole scene. I need him to be in a positive frame of mind when he's with my mom or my kids. If I complain about them, he'll try to fix it, and that always ends in disaster. I need to be guarded about what I'm feeling, particularly about those relationships. With my women friends, I can just say it all. There's this little level of guardedness with Andy that goes across everything. He sometimes takes my upsets too seriously. I don't have to worry about that with my friends."

It's often easier for us to talk with a trusted woman friend than with the person with whom we share our bed. As you may have noticed, once we become sexually involved with someone, our relationship with that person changes. Our dependency surfaces; there's an intensity; and we have expectations that rarely arise among friends. We rely on our partners in a different way than we rely on our friends. Consequently, we can usually bare our souls to a friend without risking the conflict it might bring about in a primary relationship.

While our spouses, children, or family members may have an investment in us remaining the same and may even feel threatened by our increasing independence, our friends celebrate our emerging selves. Our friends affirm and support our aspirations as well as coach us through the challenges of daily life: Should I call the principal and tell her I think she overreacted? How do I deal with my ex-husband when he brings our son home late? What to do about the debilitating sleep deprivation that I'm going through because of menopause? How do I convince my husband not to make financial decisions without consulting me? Should I buy the outfit I put on hold, even if it is out of my budget?

Our friends are sounding boards; they're a safe harbor, in which we can freely explore our most irrational and outrageous thoughts. Before my friend Celeste or I go off the deep end, we warn each other by asking, "Can I be stupid now?" And the inevitable answer is, "Sure, if I can go next." As we share our struggles, sadness, insecurities, and joys, we realize that we're not alone, that we're part of a larger community of women.

When a friend asks, "How are you?" you never simply answer, "I'm fine." We feel relieved that there's a place where we can shed our inhibitions and be ourselves without worrying whether our friend is going to head for the nearest exit, change her phone number, or join the witness protection program. When we experience the acceptance of a cherished friend, we become more patient and tolerant of ourselves. Their loyalty and understanding allows us to be ourselves.

The Care and Feeding of a Friendship

Have you ever noticed that you can start a conversation with a friend feeling confused, and then, after she has genuinely listened to you, not only do you feel relieved but you find that you can think more clearly? This isn't magic. There's nothing more reassuring than being listened to. But this requires time. Each of us has to stop what we're doing and focus on what a friend is saying. We can't take our friendships for granted. We need to nurture them. Theologian Paul Tillich said, "The first duty of love is to listen." I know you're busy—everyone is—but we need to make room in our lives to connect. A steady diet of quick phone calls or rushed meetings just won't do. Our friendships need the luxury of a leisurely walk, a quiet dinner. They need space in which we can unwind and share.

Yet some women have such demanding schedules that they find it difficult to tend to their friendships. Tory, a forty-eighty-year-old nurse practitioner, said during one of our sessions, "I don't have enough time for my friends. My life is crammed full of family and work, and when I think about all those things, friends come after them. I don't communicate as much as I wish I could. I have wonderful friends, and they will often reach out to me. I'm always delighted. But I'm in a phase of life when I'm working very hard at my business and I'm chairing two boards. My time is very heavily booked." One of the main issues that brought Tory to see me was how out of balance her life was. Although she loved her work, she found little time for anything else.

While Tory may feel a certain level of satisfaction in the other areas of her life, she has been missing out on the richness and support that ongoing friendships provide. "I had this difficult situation with one of my grown children come up a month or so ago," she said. "I was at a loss as to whom I could talk to. Up until then, I hadn't realized how lonely I've been." She hadn't invested much energy in her friendships, so when she needed help, she felt awkward approaching the women with whom she'd had only occasional contact. As we talked about the lack of ongoing friendships, Tory began to realize that there was an emotional void in her life. "I've been so involved in growing my business and dealing with family that I feel used up. I thought that I could get by, but this recent incident showed me otherwise."

When a woman hasn't taken the time to cultivate a circle of friends, there's often a sense of isolation, although she may not immediately be aware of it. Yet when she wants a pal to hang out with or someone to confide in, she discovers an emptiness in her life that isn't easily filled. As Tory experienced the emotional vacuum in her life, she began to shift her priorities to make time to cultivate her friendships. Establishing a supportive network takes time. We need to nurture our friendships so that when we need them, they're there. We have health insurance, car insurance, and a savings account to fall back on. Our friends are equally essential.

While there are some friendships that can sustain a lack of contact, most important relationships require an investment of time and attention. Whether our friends live down the street or in another city, we have to make an effort to remain involved. Sure, there are those women whom you don't talk to for months, but when you finally connect, it's as if no time has passed. In general, however, intimacy requires continuity. It's not that you have to talk with your friends every day, but you can't expect weeks or months to go by without contact and yet have a truly intimate friendship.

You Bring Out the Best in Me

As we share the details of our lives with another person, we not only cultivate trust but we get to know ourselves in a new way. Our women friends bring out different facets of our personalities. As writer Anaïs Nin observed, "Each friend represents a world in us, a world possibly not born until they arrive, and it is only by this meeting that a new world is born." A friend who is funny may foster our playfulness. A friend who is strong-willed may bring out our more assertive side. Another friend who's more intro-spective may inspire us to be more self-reflective.

"I have a particular kind of relationship with Trudy that I don't have with anyone else," Jillian, a forty-five-year-old freelance writer, said. "There's a way that we discuss lit-erature and ideas that's unique to that friendship. I love it. She's got a really interesting take on things. There's something that happens with her that doesn't happen anywhere else. I think that's true with each of my close women friends. A particular part of myself has a home in that friendship. And it doesn't have a home anywhere else. I surround myself with people who draw out different as-pects of me. I feel more complete from having my close women friends."

Our friends offer us different perspectives of ourselves and the world. We gain a second pair of eyes through our friendships. "Being with close female friends is like set-tling into a big armchair. You immediately feel comfortable and relax," Samantha, a forty-eight-year-old architect, said. "When you have the good fortune to really be able to see somebody and see what she is thinking and feeling and hear her reaction to things, it's like you get to live an-other life in addition to your own. But I'm living it with her with a perspective I never could have found myself. I gain entry to a new world. And you only gain that entry if the understanding and trust is great enough that you're both comfortable sharing at that level." By sharing our stories with other women, we gain an understanding of what it means to be female. Friendships enrich our lives immeasurably. They broaden our way of thinking and expand who we are.

Mellowing with Age

We have to work at our friendships. As we've had to learn to have more realistic expectations of our spouses and partners, we must also bring this mature outlook to our friendships. As we've had to accept the limitations, needs, and quirks of our spouses and partners, so, too, we must come to recognize the imperfect nature of our friendships.

Our friends, no matter how loyal, aren't always going to meet our needs. We're not going to agree with all of their choices, with their political or religious beliefs. It sometimes happens that we don't even like or approve of their choice in mates. Still, if we value the relationship, we must make room for the differences. We generally connect with someone because of our similarities, but it's often through our differences that we grow. If we can allow ourselves to accept those differences, we'll be enriched by the experience. But it takes work. We have to make room within ourselves to acknowledge our friends as they are, rather than as we would like them to be.

At midlife, many of us become less judgmental. We grow tolerant of our friends' imperfections, recognizing that they come as part of the package. We become more forgiving when they misunderstand or disappoint us and more appreciative of the qualities they do exude. As we recognize their immense value, we are more thankful for the richness they bring to our lives.

"Sally has fits," Louise, a fifty-three-year-old high school teacher, told me during our interview. "She doesn't keep them to herself, either. One just has to stay out of her way. But let me tell you, it's difficult not to get defensive. I want to throttle her or tell her off. She just gets prickly out of nowhere. But I understand her better now. I've just learned how to handle her moods. I realize that that's just her thing. I wouldn't put up with that with most people. But I made a conscious choice to keep her as a friend. I weighed the pros and cons in my mind and asked myself, Does the good outweigh the bad? And it did.

"Sally's a good person and a caring friend. She was there when my dad was dying. She was the person who took my son and had him stay with her family for a few days. She never made me feel guilty about it. She did it in such a way that it was going to be a treat for her to have him over. I will always be grateful to her for that because I needed for that not to be a burden. Those are really important things. I feel that in a true emergency, I could count on her. So she has moods. I'm going to nurture that relationship even if she's a bit bitty. Her goodness outweighs the bittiness. I'm committed to having her as my friend for the rest of my life."

At midlife, as we reassess our friendships, we recognize that we're going to have contradictory feelings about our friends. We have to make compromises and adjustments for our friends' quirks and limitations as they do with us.

Even with the best of friends, we find that there are places where we simply don't match. In fact, there are times when we wonder, How can I have this person in my life? We're just so different. We may have friends who make us crazy by consistently being late; friends who drive only the most expensive cars or wear only the latest fashions. We may have friends who refuse to make an effort to recycle; friends who think Shostakovich is a cheese. We may have friends who insist on getting nipped and tucked until any evidence of aging is erased. We may have friends whose parenting style makes us cringe. Still, despite all their foibles, we find that we're hopelessly devoted to them. In fact, if the truth be known, we'd be lost without them.

"When I was fifty-four, I was diagnosed with diabetes," Camile, a tall, striking-looking woman, said. "My husband was in fear mode. His immediate reaction was that he wanted to fix me. I kept telling him that he couldn't fix this. I needed him to be supportive and to know about the disease. To this day, he's read only one book. He still thinks that somehow I'm going to get better. When I tried to talk to him, he wouldn't listen to me. He would try to come up with solutions. It was stressing me out and making me crazy. Finally, I had to turn away and stop trying to make him understand. He went to the clinic with me for my first doctor's appointment. The entire time, he tried to tell the nurses what they should be doing. He couldn't just sit there and listen. After that, I wouldn't let him go with me. I was too uncomfortable with him there. Besides, I couldn't focus on getting the information I needed.

"My friend Alice just listened. I didn't have to be upbeat and pretend that I was getting a handle on the disease. I could say how scared and overwhelmed I felt just doing what I had to do to stay alive. I couldn't keep those feelings inside. I couldn't turn to Frank, because it would just scare him more. My women friends could take in how I felt and just be supportive without judging or trying to fix me. They were just there.

"One of the most reassuring things about this whole experience was Alice's speaking in terms of 'we.' '*We* have a lot to figure out,' she would say. 'But, *we'll* get through this.' I can't tell you what that meant to me. There was something so comforting about her thinking of it as her struggle, as well. Sure, I have to take care of myself, but knowing that she's in it with me is incredible.

"Alice volunteered to go with me to my doctor's appointments. She took notes. She wrote down everything. It was wonderful to have that second pair of ears. It was too much information for me to comprehend all at once. Alice would go home and transcribe her notes and just leave them on my desk for me. I would read them and discover things that the doctor had said which had flown right by me during the appointments. It was very special."

Because Camile's friend didn't feel the same kind of emotional charge or threat that Frank felt, she was able to be more objective and supportive. Whether we're married or single, our women friends are essential in helping us through a crisis. Any situation, no matter how difficult, becomes more tolerable when we feel we're not alone. When someone understands our sadness and pain, our load is lightened. Most of the women I interviewed expressed, in one way or another, that they wouldn't have made it through the difficult experiences in their lives without their close women friends.

As writer Maya Angelou observes, "In times of trouble, there are about seven women in the United States I can call at any hour and say, 'Now. Now. I need you now.' And they will come. No questions. No objections . . . Nothing, nothing would keep them from me and me from them."

One of the most sacred experiences we can have is when a friend trusts us with her vulnerability. Think about it: It's truly an honor to share that level of intimacy with another human being. When we reveal ourselves to our closest friends and they stand by us, we experience a sense of acceptance and understanding. They know our imperfections, but they also see our strengths. Our close friends often know us better than we know ourselves.

Gal Pals

Many of us become overly serious during this time of our lives. We work hard at our careers, raise our children, care for aging parents, and as a result, our playful, fun side often gets lost in the shuffle. Play is an essential ingredient for our health and longevity. And yet it's something we are apt to overlook. Our women friends often prove to be some of our best playmates.

Here are just a few examples of what women do with their friends. Rita, who is married and has two teenage children, has a weekly date with other married women to go salsa dancing. Lauren took her friend to a Bruce Springsteen concert for her fiftieth birthday, then went to a karaoke bar and sang Bruce's songs, out of tune but with reckless abandon. Toni meets Natalie five mornings a week to walk. Judith's friend Pam left her son with her husband and rented a red Mustang convertible: they drove down the California coast with the top down. My friend Valarie and I call each other "Hanz" and "Franz" (you remember the muscle men on *Saturday Night Live*). We meet at the gym three afternoons a week to work out. It keeps us honest about showing up and makes the work-out much more fun.

"My friend Eleanor is ten years older than I am," Natasha, a fifty-eight-year-old music company executive, said. "I look to her a lot because she's still such a kid at heart. She has such a wonderful, positive attitude. I have a tendency to fall into a black hole when I get stressed-out or worried. Eleanor always has a way of talking me through it. When I'm with her, I feel surrounded by her love and her humor. She can be a little girl and giggle, and she be-comes ageless at that point. She has a sparkle in her eye when she's telling me that she's had an unclean thought about some nineteen-year-old guy or something. She's al-most seventy years old and she has such a zest for life. I try hard every day to be like that. She has made a con-scious effort to live life to its fullest.

"Eleanor and I travel together. Sometimes my husband is with us, and that makes for comments from other peo-ple. We pretend that we're wife number one and wife number two. She and I have gone to New York to go to the museums. We took off last Christmas and went to a spa in Mexico together. A few years ago, we went to New York with a group to see Broadway shows. While we were there, we went ice-skating in Central Park. We were quite a sight, clinging to one another as we stumbled around the rink. But we had a ball."

Our friendships take many forms. Sometimes we mother one another. Sometimes we are the sister we always wished we'd had. When was the last time you made a date with one of your gal pals to do something fun? What are you waiting for?

Remember When

At midlife, women become more appreciative of having known one another over time, of having a shared history. The continuity of knowing someone through boyfriends, husbands, careers, and children becomes more precious as we age. Earlier in our lives, we relied on our parents to hold that memory. But at midlife, we often turn to our friends to hold us in their hearts and minds.

"Roz has been there through most of the major events in my adult life," Kathleen, a fifty-two-year-old divorce attorney, said. "She was there for my daughter's high school and college graduations, through my divorce, the deaths of my brother and mother, the opening of my business. She's been a constant in my life. She's not that fond of her sister, and I don't have one. So we've said this is the sister relationship. It feels like that. It's like having a sister because of the longevity. The fact that we've known each other over the past twenty-eight years makes it different from any of my other friendships. We've known virtually all the players in each other's lives."

Another woman, Bianca, said, "I have one friend whom I've known for thirty-two years. She was my friend in college and is actually my ex-sister-in-law. We know people in common who have been powerful for both of us, particularly her parents, her grandparents, my ex-husband. We've remained close to each other through all the ups and downs. We help to interpret the world that we've shared—the marriages, children, personal ambitions, hopes for careers, interpreting our growing up and how we felt."

There's something wonderfully heartwarming about being able to say, "Remember that time when . . ." There's something reassuring abut having someone who has known us through the different phases of our lives and has seen us grow. There's a shorthand that exists between long-term friends in which little has to be explained— they just know. There's an ease that exists between women who have known each other over time, who have weathered crisis, challenges, heartbreak. Old friends provide a memory bank. We have a pretty good idea of how we are going to react and we can remind one another of how we coped with situations in the past. There's a trust that only time and experience can bring.

We Can Work It Out, at Least Most of the Time

Even the best of friends encounter rough spots from time to time. It comes with the territory. No friendship, at least not one of any depth, is going to be conflict-free. In case you haven't noticed, we're complex beings. At midlife, when we've made a commitment to express our thoughts, feelings, and needs more honestly, we're bound to disappoint occasionally or hurt a friend's feelings. Besides, if we're truthful, we each have our own special brand of craziness that causes rifts to occur. It's not that we fall into the rabbit hole from time to time that can make or break a friendship, it's what we do to mend the situation.

"Tanya had been living in our guest house for three

years rent-free," Jenny, a fifty-five-year-old sculptor, said. "We had put our house on the market and within the first week we got an offer. Tanya had volunteered to help me pack up, which was going to be a monumental task. My husband and I went on an exploratory trip to California to look for a new house. When we returned, she had moved all of her things out of the guest house. I was angry. I couldn't believe that she would just flake out on me when I really needed her. But she did. By the time Tanya finally called, we were almost done. After much wrestling with myself, I just let the whole thing go.

"A few months after we were settled in our new house, she wrote me a long letter. She apologized and explained what had happened. She told me how much she appreciated my friendship and how sorry she was for what she'd done. For me, when someone has the courage to say, 'I screwed up. I'm sorry, I made a mistake,' that's all it takes. I realized that there will always be a bond between us. Age has enabled me to clarify what I want to preserve and what I want to let go of. And my friendship with Tanya was well worth saving."

The best friends are the ones with whom you can talk out your differences. But this goes against everything we've been taught. You know the drill: Women are supposed to be nice, conciliatory, blah, blah, blah. Baloney, we can't afford this any longer. Not only is it unhealthy but it will create distance between us if we don't risk talking about our feelings, and this can sink a friendship. True friendship demands courage—the willingness to hang in there and wrestle with one another. When we do, we learn not only that we can withstand conflict, which is always scary, but that our friendship is strengthened by having weathered the storm. At midlife, we require greater authenticity in all areas of our lives—friendships included. At midlife, we're no longer willing to allow our thoughts, feelings, and needs to go unexpressed. We're no longer willing to settle for less than honest, forthright relationships—be it with ourselves, at work, with our spouses, or with our friends.

While Tanya and Jenny were able to work through a difficult time in their friendship, this isn't always the case. In the reevaluation that occurs during midlife, we sometimes discover that as much as we may have valued a particular friend, we've either grown apart or the friendship no longer meets our needs. Just as we have demanded equality in our primary relationships, we also want it with our friends. If a friend can't allow us to grow beyond our role of caretaker, if she refuses to do the internal soul-searching that is essential to negotiate this passage successfully, we often decide that the friendship isn't worth continuing. While breaking off a friendship may be painful, most women can no longer tolerate friends with whom they can't share the journey.

"I've found myself sorting, saying, Whom can I be totally myself with? Who supports me? Whom do I trust and feel safe with? That's become my criteria," Petra, a fifty-one-year-old stylist, said. "This person yes, this person no. I'm choosing whom I want to have in my life. A lot of it has to do with shared values. You know with someone if there's room to bring all of yourself into the friendship. I love Jean. We've known each other for twenty-one years, since our daughters were three. I've tried to talk to her about things other than the most superficial details of my life and she gets uncomfortable. I feel there's not room for all of who I am, and I just can't censor myself anymore. I think that was the death knell for the friendship. I still care about her and probably always will. She was important during a particular time in my life. But I just found that I don't put any energy into keeping in touch. My time is full, and I only want people in my life whom I can be real with."

Some of our friendships will last a lifetime. We can endure the changes of midlife together and discover an ability to grow with one another. But there are other friendships that will not survive this passage. For a multitude of reasons, we either cannot or choose not to work out the problems. In these cases, we must recognize and appreciate what we've shared while honoring our need to move on.

The Truth, the Whole Truth, and Nothing but the Truth

As with anyone we love, there are times when our caring is expressed through empathy and understanding. Yet there are other times when a friend is so caught up in a situation that she can't see clearly. At those times, we have to find the courage to tell the truth, even when we know that it may not be what our friend wants to hear. Being able to say the hard things is a sign of genuine love. While our friends may not be thrilled, they do count on us for our clarity, honesty, and, at times, to give them a good swift kick in the butt.

"I tend to give people the benefit of the doubt," Barbara, a fifty-three-year-old psychologist, said. "Even after I found out that my husband was cheating on me, I can remember feeling these glimmers of hope. I had this fantasy that Paul would acknowledge and take responsibility for what he'd done. He'd written me this wonderful letter. He told me that he was ready to be a devoted husband. Well, I was starting to buy it. I wanted so much for it to work between us. I remember telling my friend Alexandra that I thought Paul was coming around. There was dead silence on the other end of the phone. Then she reminded me that he'd said all these things before and nothing had changed. She told me that I was going to settle for crumbs, that Paul didn't treat me the way I deserved to be treated. She was actually angrier than I was."

I asked Barbara how she felt about her friend telling her these things. "In the moment, it wasn't fun to be confronted. I got mad at her for saying those things about Paul. But before long, I came around. I couldn't stay in denial. When you hear something that your soul knows is the truth, there's something about it that brings you closer to your real self. It feels good. It's not fun, but I crave it. I need that and want that from my friends. It's what Paul and I could never do with each other. I count on my friends to tell me the truth. I know that they're doing it from a place of caring and I value that."

Sometimes, we have to voice the thoughts and feelings that our friends can't express themselves. Poet Adrienne Rich conveyed this when she wrote, "An honorable human relationship—that is, one which . . . people have the right to use the word love—is a process, delicate, violent, often terrifying . . . a process of refining truths they can tell each other. It is important to do this because it breaks down self-delusion and isolation. . . . It is important to do this because we can count on so few people to go that hard way with us."

Telling the truth is a sign of our devotion and commitment to a friendship. During midlife, when our identity is in flux and we often feel lost, our friends provide support and validation. As we struggle to redefine ourselves, our women friends become that much more essential—to act as beacons, to explore what's most meaningful in our lives, to share our heartaches and triumphs, to inspire us to fulfill our deepest longings. Our soul sisters help us to discover and reclaim our true selves.

At midlife, many of us find that we're drawn toward other women whose lives are inspired by a similar quest—women who are wrestling with the deeper issues and questions of life, women who are seeking greater authenticity, women who are pursuing their dreams, women with whom we share the joys and struggles of the journey.

Chapter 9

GIVING BIRTH TO OURSELVES

i found god in myself & i loved her/ i loved her fiercely.

—NTOZAKE SHANGE

Chances are that if I asked you who you are, you'd tell me your name, age, your marital status. You would tell me about your family, your career, your interests, favorite books, music, movies. But the truth is, you are more than all of this. You are more than what you do, the roles you play, what you own, what you love. Deep within our being resides our soul—our connection with the Infinite. It's what we bring with us when we are born, and it's what exists after we're gone. While our personality and body change with time, our soul remains the same. It's always with us, but we're usually unaware of its presence. The din of the world makes it difficult for us to hear the "still small voice" that represents the depths of our being.

As young women, most of us sought our identity and fulfillment in the everyday world, and for the first half of our lives, that was appropriate. Yet at midlife, we sense that there must be something more. We've expended so much of our energy seeking material rewards that we've overlooked the importance of our inner life. It's not that our authentic self has abandoned us; we've simply lost sight of it. Our inner being is there, intact, waiting for us to return. At midlife, we yearn to bring this sacred dimension into our lives.

During this passage, we often experience a homesickness—a dissatisfaction with our lives. We realize that the world is not our true home, that something's missing. We feel like a stranger in a strange land who's longing to return to her roots. We blame our discontent on a lack of fulfillment in our careers, relationships, or families, when in truth it's a longing to return to something more essential—to reconnect with our soul. The feelings of dissatisfaction are a catalyst not just for psychological growth but for spiritual growth, as well. Many of the women I interviewed spoke of a desire for greater depth in their lives. As we enter the second half of our lives, we're called to explore our internal world. It's not that we haven't done this before, but now we have the life experience and maturity to appreciate its importance. Many of us have achieved a certain amount of success, yet we realize that the peace and satisfaction we've longed for must now come from within. Carl Jung wrote that the essential question for the second half of our lives is whether we are "related to something infinite or not." This requires that we make a commitment to reconnect with our deeper nature.

The Turn Within

There is a famous Indian story about an argument between the gods over where to hide the secret of life.

"Bury it under a mountain," one god suggested. "They'll never find it there."

"No," the other countered, "one day they will find a way to dig up the mountain and uncover the secret of life."

"Put it in the depths of the ocean," another god suggested. "It will be safe there."

"No," said the others, "someday humankind will find a way to travel to the depths of the ocean and will find it."

"Put it inside them," another god said. "Men and women will never think of looking for it there."

All the gods agreed, and so it is said that the gods hid the secret of life within us.

Who would have thought that the very thing we've been seeking is as close as our own breath? The great thinkers throughout history have offered us their guidance. Diogenes implored, "Know thyself"; Shakespeare said, "To thine own self be true"; Plato cautioned, "The unexamined life is not worth living"; and Jesus advised his followers, "The Kingdom of God is within you." Now it's time to make a conscious choice. Are we going to continue to search for more and more achievement in the world or are we going to search for the deeper meaning of our lives?

One of the essential challenges of this midlife transition is how we can remain actively involved in the world while maintaining our connection to an inner life. This isn't easy, especially in our materially oriented society, where a person's worth is measured by what we own, whom we know, how much power we wield, rather than by the quality of our being. But at midlife, when we've been stripped of much of what we believed in, we feel compelled to ponder the mysteries, to wrestle with the larger questions: Where do I stand in the greater scheme of things? What is my purpose? Who am I really? What is the meaning of my life? These timeless questions suddenly become more pressing, less theoretical. Now, rather than looking to an authority figure for the answers, we must search within ourselves. And while we may not be able to answer all of those questions, the act of engaging in the inquiry will enrich our lives.

At midlife, our inner ground shifts. Our ego takes a backseat and our authentic self becomes our center of gravity—our reason for being. We can no longer afford to allow our fears or the need to prove ourselves to continue to drive us. Many of us feel an urgency to reassess our motivation. I certainly did.

I had already felt a vague sense of dissatisfaction with my life and then my mother died suddenly. I was forty-six years old, and my world tipped off its axis. I had just spent the previous year and a half pouring my energy into a television project, only to have it canceled two weeks before shooting. I had had such high expectations of what this was going to do for my career that when it all came crashing down, I became disillusioned and depressed.

Until that time, I had thought that my need for success was normal—in fact, admirable. But following my mother's death, I began to wonder why I had pushed myself so hard, why I had continually strived for ever-greater recognition. No matter what I accomplished, why did I need to do more?

During the days and months that I mourned the loss of my mother, it began to dawn on me that I had always been a doer. In fact, looking back, I recognized that I had been a type A toddler. Without having realized it, much of what I had done had been motivated by a need to prove myself, to show my parents, the world, myself that I was worthwhile. On some level, I was continually trying to justify my existence, as if I weren't good enough and that I had to make up for some huge personal deficit. Don't get me wrong, it's not that I hadn't done good work. But I was never satisfied. It finally occurred to me that I had been looking in the wrong place.

Like so many of the women I spoke with, I wanted something deeper to be the guiding force in my life. I yearned to let go, to do what had always been so difficult for me—to trust. As frightened as I was, I wanted to find out what would happen if I stopped pushing so hard. It's not that I wanted to give up what I had been doing—that wasn't even a consideration. I wanted my motivation to be different. I wanted to surrender to the river of my life and allow its current to carry me. I wanted whatever it was that I was going to do to be motivated from the deepest place I could find within me. Anything else would be intolerable.

I began to do something I'd never done before: I began to pray. I still can't tell you whom or what I pray to, but every morning I give thanks for all that I have in my life and then I ask "to do thy will above my will." Then I sit and focus on my breathing and watch the zillions of mundane thoughts float through my mind. This time has become my anchor. It sets the tone for the day. It helps me to connect with something larger than myself. It helps me to keep things in perspective, at least most of the time. I'm not going to pretend that I haven't had my moments of panic—well, maybe more than moments. Committing

ourselves to a deeper calling is a major shift for most of us.
It's certainly not something that we're going to find a lot
of support for in our culture. But when we make the commitment to respond from the core of our being, a burden
is lifted. When we finally admit that we don't have all the
answers and we surrender to something deeper, we experience a tremendous sense of relief. What we choose to do
in the world will be a natural outgrowth of this connection
with our soul. It will emerge from the deepest sense of
who we are.

When we pray, we're declaring a sacred intention. We're
reaching out across the universe and giving voice to our
deepest longings. Prayer is our attempt at communion with
a higher power—be it God, Goddess, nature spirits, or the
place that connects us to a larger wisdom. When we pray, we
enter into a dialogue with this other; we open ourselves to a
wiser voice. Meditation serves a different need. Meditation
is a process of observation, of centering. It's a quieting of the
mind, a time of introspection, a time when we can achieve a
dispassionate distance from which to look at our dreams,
fears, and the concerns that occupy our attention. In meditation, we have an opportunity to drop below the turbulence
of our lives and connect with the calm place within us.

Do-Be-Do-Be-Do-Be-Do

I know this was what the Shirelles, the Crystals, and the
Ronettes sang in the 1950s and Frank Sinatra sang in the
1960s, but it's also one of the greatest challenges in our
lives. To be or to do, and how to strike a balance, is the all
important question. Our culture abhors idleness. The

adage "Idle hands are the Devil's workshop" grew out of the Puritan ethic of keeping busy. Yet, contrary to popular belief, taking time to meditate or pray isn't the same as being lazy—quite the opposite, in fact. Both require discipline and dedication.

"Certainly, the attitude I was raised with was to be a worker," Zoie, a forty-nine-year-old professor of English literature, told me. "I'm a doer, a human doer. I think if you had a hidden camera in my house watching me alone, you'd see that I'm like a jack-in-the-box. I'll sit down to be quiet and then I pop up. I've been one of those people who was always busy. That was so embedded in me that I've had a hard time shaking it. I don't feel right if I'm not doing. If I decide I want just to sit and look out the window or spend the morning in bed, I'm aware that there's something inside of me that says, You're lazy. You know that you've got tenure papers that you have to finish up, or you need to be working on that article. It goes on and on. I've gotten better, but it's still a struggle."

A number of the women I spoke with echoed this sentiment. They struggle to be able to take time for themselves, to focus on what's going on inside. Several women confessed that they felt like they were cheating when they "did nothing." They felt that they had to get sick in order to have an excuse to take time for themselves. Yet if we adhere to society's dictates to do, do, do, we become automatons and lose touch with our humanity.

There are other ways for us to measure ourselves. The king of Bhutan, for example, has decided that rather than encouraging his citizens to aspire to a higher gross national product, he would measure what he called "gross national happiness." Tibetan culture has always assigned greater value to being rather than to how much one accomplishes. It's no wonder so many of us have been attracted to its ethics and religion.

Most of us live as if we are careening down a freeway. Think about how much you miss when you're traveling at warp speed. We need to take the first available exit and pull into a quiet country lane, slow down, and reflect on our lives. There is a saying in Thailand: Life is so short— we must move very slowly. But slowing down requires courage and commitment. It means swimming against the societal tide. As we cross into the second half of our lives, we must learn when to do and when to be. How to strike a vibrant balance between the two becomes crucial.

The Sounds of Silence

Our society doesn't encourage solitude. For women especially, it's considered taboo. Our culture considers solitude wasted, unproductive time. When we do take time for ourselves, we're considered selfish, as if a certain amount of self-care isn't healthy. People who spend time alone are often accused of being self-absorbed, narcissistic. When we dare to spend "too much" time alone, people, especially people close to us, often feel uncomfortable. They take it as a rejection or they assume that something's wrong with us. Unfortunately, many of us have bought into this notion. When we feel the need to withdraw, we think of ourselves as weird or neurotic. We convince ourselves that there's more to do and that we can't possibly justify being idle.

It should come as no surprise that many women often experience feelings of anxiety when it comes to taking time for themselves. After all, we place tremendous value on relationships. Some women I spoke with considered being alone only slightly better than being sentenced to solitary confinement. They couldn't understand why someone would choose to spend time away from other people and activity. Yet the truth is, if we're not connected with our inner self, no amount of love is going to provide the comfort we seek. We'll try to fill ourselves up with food, shopping, alcohol, work, or relationships, but it will not satisfy our hunger—our desire to connect with the sacred. That can happen only when we turn our attention inward, when we become comfortable with ourselves.

Solitude is the crucible for the emerging self. It provides us with time to reflect on our day, our past, our future, our dreams. Time alone is essential if we're going to discover the larger purpose of our lives. Yet the goal of solitude is not to become a self-centered navel-gazer. Far from it. In turning inward, we experience renewal. We cultivate a more essential vision. When we do return to our daily lives, we do so with a new focus.

Poet May Sarton writes in her book *Journal of a Solitude*, "Here I am alone for the first time in weeks, to take up my 'real' life again at last. That is what is strange—that friends, even passionate lovers, are not my real life unless there is time alone in which to explore and to discover what is happening or has happened. Without the interruptions, nourishing and maddening, this life would become arid. Yet I taste it fully only when I am alone here and the house and I resume old conversations."

As I read through the interviews I conducted, I was amazed to find how many different forms of solitude these women had adopted. Here are just a few of the creative ways women have found to nourish their souls.

Diana, a forty-six-year-old artist: "I get up really early in the morning before everyone is awake. I have a need for time alone, and it's difficult to manage being a parent three times over. I'm careful with what I do during this time because it's so valuable and precious to me. I go out into the garden and I study every bud, every petal on my roses. Then I cut off the dead flowers. It's a form of meditation and renewal."

Kathleen, a fifty-one-year-old television producer: "I've struggled to make time, but I've discovered that a little contemplation every day is as essential as food or oxygen. It doesn't have to be very long, just fifteen or twenty minutes. I make sure the answering machine is on. I have a little altar set up in the bedroom. I light a candle and just clear out all the clutter of the day until I can feel me. I never thought I'd say this, but solitude has become my best friend."

Jackie, a fifty-five-year-old policy analyst: "For me, my karate practice is a time when I'm completely in the moment. My attention is totally on what I'm doing. I can't afford to think about what happened at home or at work or even ten minutes ago, because I will have lost the precision of the move. So for three or four hours a week, that's my meditation."

Elsa, a forty-one-year-old physical therapist: "I play the piano and it takes me to a place of real quiet inside like nothing else. I can always tell when I need solitude. There's this little voice that lets me know it's time. And I go to the piano. Out of playing comes a sense of knowing who I am. Sometimes I find that I cross out an afternoon on my calendar just for me. If someone calls, I'll say, 'I have an appointment,' and it's with myself. I may write in my journal or read or just rest and do whatever I feel will recharge and reconnect me. I think I have a wellspring inside of me, and I need to connect with it. The only way to do that is for me to be alone."

Aren't you inspired? Even though these women struggled with feelings of guilt, selfishness, and inertia, they managed to make time to nourish the most essential part of themselves.

Our feelings of guilt often arise from our unrealistic expectations. You remember all those impossible ideals we set for ourselves when we were young and foolish? Well, there's still one or two of them lurking around in the background, continuing to wreak havoc. The good news is that there is something we can do. We can either adjust our standards so that they more closely match reality or we can change our behavior. In most cases, I would suggest trashing those ridiculous expectations. Let the air out of the larger-than-life-size version of yourself and admit that you are a mere human who has needs of her own. Then go about overcoming the inertia that causes you to maintain the status quo. Anyone who's ever tried to institute an exercise program or to modify her eating habits knows just what a challenge it is to do something new. Start small, do what feels manageable, but make the commitment and carve out the time for yourself. Sure, it will feel awkward at first—everything new does—but stick with it and before long I guarantee that you'll be fanatically protective of your alone time.

Nobel Prize–winning poet Juan Ramón Jiménez recognized this when he wrote the poem "I AM NOT I":

I am not I.
          I am this one
walking beside me whom I do not see,
whom at times I manage to visit,
and whom at other times I forget;
who remains calm and silent while I talk,
and forgives, gently, when I hate,
who walks where I am not,
who will remain standing when I die.

Learning to Listen

I know, you must be wondering what I'm talking about when I suggest that we have to learn how to listen. After all, we listen to ourselves all the time—we know when we're hungry or tired. We know when we're too hot or too cold. But that's not what I'm talking about. That's Listening 101. I'm suggesting a more challenging course of study, where we learn to quiet the racket of our minds so that we can discover the voice of the soul. It's a lot like sending a listening device into the depths of the ocean to locate hidden treasure. We have to go below the fracas of the world that we carry around on the surface of our consciousness to find what resides within the deepest recesses of our beings. But this is no easy task.

Quieting one's mind is a lot like trying to get a roomful of toddlers to settle down. No, it isn't impossible. It can be done, but it requires practice and discipline and it's a practice well worth cultivating.

"A little more than a year ago, I started to block out time just to sit and be quiet. I realized that I didn't spend much time praying or meditating," Lois, a blond fifty-one-year-old movie executive, told me as we sat in her office. "With all the mind chatter going on, I couldn't hear things. I have this voice that's really very helpful. It guides me in the right direction. But I also have these other voices that are screaming, I've gotta do this, or Why haven't I done that? They drown it out. By sitting, I've learned how to quiet my mind.

"My dreams have become important tools for me. I never used to remember them, but now I keep a pad and pen next to my bed and I write them down first thing when I wake up. The other night, I had a dream that I was walking on the ocean floor. I could see the crustaceans, the coral, beautiful rainbow fish. There was a mountain underneath the ocean, and I accidentally stepped off the edge. The bottom of the ocean just dropped out. When I landed on the floor, I realized that I was on a new level."

I asked Lois what she thought her dream meant. "I think that I've gone deeper in my life. In the past few months, I've been paying closer attention to my insides, which isn't exactly easy in the crazy world of the entertainment industry. I feel really quiet inside, peaceful. I'm in a place of gathering, observing, listening. I started to get what I call faxes from God."

" 'Faxes from God'?" I asked.

"Yeah, when I'm sitting in contemplation, I get these messages that I can't ignore. When I first started sitting, it felt like I had plaque on my channels, but after a few weeks, it was like the arteries suddenly opened up. Something deeper began to speak to me. No, it isn't like the *Exorcist* or channeling some four-thousand-year-old entity. It's this wise place in me, the place that knows. I've learned to trust it. I can be in the middle of a stressful meeting, and I say to myself, Faxing, faxing. Come in. Hello, hello. And then I just listen, and inevitably I know what to do. I've made an absolute commitment to follow the faxes, whether in business or in personal situations. It's never failed me. It's become the guiding force in my life."

Before the days of baby monitors, mothers used to keep one ear tuned to their sleeping child in the next room. We have to listen to ourselves with the same attentiveness. Yet many women are afraid of what they might hear when they truly listen. Even if feelings of sadness or despair percolate out of the stillness, it is ultimately good news. I know you might be saying to yourself, What is she, nuts? Why would I want to make room in my life for those unpleasant feelings? Our feelings are messengers. They're there for a reason. We need to know how we feel. We need to hear how tired we are, how disappointed or disillusioned, how stressed or bored. It's only when we listen that we can recognize what's out of balance in our lives. What we discover may lead us to make different choices. But even when it doesn't, we will likely achieve greater clarity and purpose.

We must create time in our lives in which to be with ourselves. Don't panic. I'm not suggesting that you join a convent. What I am saying is that it's essential that you make time for yourself *every day*. Yes, every day. Let's put things in perspective. You feed yourself three times a day. Time alone is food for your soul. It may be only ten or fifteen minutes. That's fine. But you need time to quiet your ordinary voice so that you can hear the language of your heart. In the silence, a woman can learn to discern whom to trust, which path to take, when to move forward and when to wait, when to make others a priority and when to focus on herself.

Solitude is necessary for our psychological and spiritual

health. It's only in silence that we can connect with our inner knowing. In the silence, we can discover the treasure of who we are. In silence, our soul whispers her wisdom. In the silence, we discover her secrets. At midlife, when we're at a crossroads, we need silence in order to hear the pulsing of our own lives. Make a commitment to yourself and find a private place where you won't be disturbed, and then practice listening.

A Room of One's Own

In 1929, the British writer Virginia Woolf published *A Room of One's Own,* based on two lectures that she had delivered the previous year at Cambridge University. In her presentation, she expressed a fact that women had acknowledged for years: In order for a woman to be creative, she requires privacy. Woolf's famous dictum is as true today as when she first wrote it. Women need to have a space of their own—a sanctuary apart from the rest of their lives. It's difficult to detach from the demands of family, friends, and work. We often feel compelled to remain involved in the activities of the world unless we physically remove ourselves from our everyday surroundings.

Women have become such experts at supporting and mirroring others that without a place of our own, it's often difficult, though not impossible, to experience our essential self. "I've created a space for myself in a spare bedroom. It's behind the laundry room, so it's quite separate from the rest of the house," Audrey, a forty-nine-year-old vocal accompanist and mother of two teenage daughters, said. "It's wonderful. It's my special place. Because I have a full-time husband and two children, I needed a space that I can call mine. When I go there and close the door, it's a clear signal to everybody that I don't want to be disturbed. I don't want their presence in my room unless they're invited. I don't want to know who's on the phone. I don't want to know what my children want. I'm just there. One of the biggest problems for me is that I really do run the household. If anything needs doing, guess who gets the job?

"I explained to my family, 'I love you all dearly, but I really need time away from you when I'm not a mother, a wife, a singer, I'm just me.' It took a bit of doing, but eventually they respected it. I've furnished my room very sparsely, unlike the rest of our house. I have bookshelves filled with my books and little treasures from when I was a volunteer in South America. Sometimes all I do is sit and watch the leaves on the ficus tree outside my window move. That's it. If I feel like writing and something comes forth, I do that. Having my own room just allows me to tune in to me, separate and apart from anything or anybody. I've come to realize that not only is it essential, it's absolutely delicious."

Audrey is fortunate to have a spare room, but not all of us can allocate that much space to ourselves. When my daughter was still living at home, I took a cardboard box, covered it with a shawl my brother had given me from Bali, and put it in a corner. That was my sacred space. A room of one's own can be anyplace where you create a private space for yourself—a corner, a windowsill, a bench in a secluded garden. What's important is that you make a place that is yours and yours alone.

The scholar and mythologist Joseph Campbell often talked about the value of having a "sacred place." He wrote:

This is an absolute necessity for anybody today. You must have a room, or a certain hour or so a day, where you don't know what was in the newspapers that morning, you don't know who your friends are, you don't know what you owe anybody, you don't know what anybody owes to you. This is a place where you can simply experience and bring forth what you are and what might be. This is a place of creative incubation. At first you may find nothing happens there. But if you have a sacred place and use it, something eventually will happen.

Sacred Ordinariness

At midlife, we are being asked to undergo a shift in consciousness. When we were young, we could afford to separate spirituality from the practical. Many of the women I interviewed discovered that their sense of spirituality has evolved over the years. Whether women have returned to the religion of their childhood or have found a sense of the Infinite in nature, Buddhism, Christianity, or the Cabala, they all have one thing in common: Their spirituality is no longer something they devote themselves to only on Sunday, when they attend church, or on Friday night, when they light the Sabbath candles. It now encompasses their lives, moment by moment, day by day.

Our spirituality is now about our relationship with the sacred—with a greater reality that gives our life meaning—and how we bring that connection into our everyday activities. It is our quest to become more genuine. It is the awareness of how interdependent we are. In midlife, we recognize that within the mundane, the extraordinary often exists. Whether it's washing the dishes, making love, talking with the mechanic at the gas station, we can make sacred everything we do, by investing it with attentiveness and compassion. But like anything else, we must recommit ourselves daily. It's not something we do once and then forget about it. It's like strengthening any other muscle. It requires regular exercise.

"My parents were demanding churchgoers. When I grew up, I couldn't go out on a Saturday night unless I went to church on Sunday," Claudia, a fifty-four-year-old software product manager, said. "During my twenties, when the Vietnam War and the civil rights protests were going on, I broke from the church. I began to question traditional religion. I've tried to find my own sense of spirituality. It's not at all form-based. It's very internal. My spirituality has become very practical.

"Last year, I went on a weekend-long silent retreat. I left feeling inspired. I began to see that God was in everything—in the food I cook for my family, the laundry I wash, the good-night kisses I give my son and daughter. It seems foolish that we should think that God is present only in a house of worship and not everywhere, in everything. I try to keep that in my mind. It's become a form of meditation. I say to myself, This, too, is God—the girl at the check-out counter is God; the guy who just cut me off is also God. I try to take the time to validate each person's humanness and see the sacredness in all things. I don't want you to think that you're talking to Mother Teresa. Far from it. I lose it regularly. I scream at the drivers on the freeway and regularly at my kids, but all in all, reminding myself that everything is sacred helps me to keep a spiritual focus in my life."

At midlife, we must make every aspect of our lives sacred so that our lives become our spiritual practice. There's a wonderful story about Mahatma Gandhi. He was riding on a train that was pulling out of the station. A reporter rushed up to him and said, "Bapu, please give me a message to take back to the people." Gandhi quickly wrote a note on a scrap of paper and thrust it into the man's hand. It said, "My life is my message." I ask you to consider what message you are sending with your life. And what do you want the message of your life to be? Remember, everything we do matters—absolutely everything, no matter how small or insignificant. We must live as if this is true. When we do, our lives become our spiritual practice.

Recognizing the Stories We Live By

As we take time to listen, we have an opportunity to better understand where we reside in the story of our lives. Every experience we've had, no matter how painful or delightful, has contributed to the fabric of the person we are today. It's time to look back, not with a critical eye, but, rather, to discover the connecting thread that gives our lives rhythm and meaning. Our past reminds us of challenges we've endured, the strengths we've accumulated, and the wisdom we've extracted from our experiences. By recalling our lives, we re-collect ourselves. We gather together forgotten priorities and passions.

"I was at a party with people I'd known since 1969, most of whom I hadn't seen in years," Laurel, a forty-five-year-old social worker, said. "It was incredibly reassuring. I'd been a bit nervous about going. In the past, I'd usually come away from something like that and feel bad. I would've compared myself to the women who were still married, or who were more successful or something. But believe it or not, this time I didn't feel like I should be someone else.

"Remember those puzzles in the children's magazine *Highlights* where you'd connect all the dots to make a picture? Well, after the party, as I lay in bed thinking about all that I've done, the choices I've made, where I am in my life now, it was like connecting the dots of my life. It felt like my life was coming into focus. And it was an awfully good feeling.

"Sure, there are regrets, but I feel like I'm laying to rest the disappointments of not having fulfilled some of the idealized images I had of myself and some of the expectations that I didn't meet. There are things I wished I might have done differently, but I know myself well enough that if I was given ten chances, I probably wouldn't have been able to do it any other way. That acceptance is very comforting.

"I used to compare myself to my older sister. She has an important position in a mental-health organization in New York. I was constantly thinking that I wasn't doing enough, that I should be presenting papers at conferences, trying to become more visible. But as I've started to really listen to myself, I realize not only that it's not something I like doing but that the comparisons diminished my appreciation for who I am and what I've done. I've spent so much of my life doing what needed to be done—raising my family and building my counseling practice. Now, if anything, I want to pursue my own interests, like taking some lessons in traditional Irish dancing, rather than invest more time in my well-established career."

As Laurel took stock of her life, she gained greater self-respect. The word *respect* is derived from the Greek *respectar,* which means "the willingness to look again." We need to be willing to look again at ourselves—choices made, paths not taken, dreams left undone—and have the courage to claim all of it as our own. As novelist Thomas Wolfe wrote in *Look Homeward, Angel,* "I am part of all that I have touched and that has touched me." In order to live an authentic life, we must integrate all of our experiences and relationships. We must recognize that regardless of whether they were painful or joyful, we are richer for having had them. As we take stock of our lives, we're better able to move forward with increased confidence and a greater sense of who we are.

While some women may consider it indulgent to look back, the transformation that occurs at midlife demands that we see where we've been and how far we've come. We need to remember in order to preserve our wholeness. We need to remember in order to see ourselves clearly.

When we understand our own stories, we learn that the past no longer holds us prisoner, that we can recast our present and create a future from carefully chosen goals and ideals. Now is the time to give birth to ourselves.

Giving Birth to Ourselves

At midlife, we are not being asked to reinvent ourselves. We are being called upon to give birth to what is hidden deep within us. In a Hasidic tale, Rabbi Zusya, who is about to die, announces to his followers, "When I meet my maker I will not be asked why I was not Moses. I shall be asked why I was not Zusya?"

That is the question for each of us. Why aren't we the person we were intended to be? Why do we try to be someone other than ourselves? As we cross this threshold into the second half of our lives, we can no longer continue to try to be who our parents expected us to become, what our spouse or children want us to be, what our culture prescribes for us. We must envision the entirety of who we are and bring forth what is true and real about ourselves.

At midlife, we insist that our lives be all of a piece—we want there to be a thread of genuineness that runs through all of our relationships. We don't want to act one way with colleagues and another way at home. We don't want to feel one way and act another. We want the person on the inside to match the person in the outer world. We want to feel integrated—whole.

No, this doesn't happen overnight. Just as it requires nine months for a baby to come to term, we, too, need a period of gestation. For those of us who have experienced being pregnant, we can recall how we needed additional rest, care, and nourishment as the new life was growing within our wombs. The same holds true today; only the life we are birthing now is our own. We must now lavish the same devotion, nurturing, and attention on ourselves. We must act as our own mothers and midwives as we give birth to the mature adult woman who is emerging.

I realize that many of us haven't had the benefit of thoughtful, caring mothering throughout our lives. Consequently, it's often difficult to care for our own needs. But despite our earlier experiences, midlife offers us a rare opportunity to make a commitment to cherish and nourish ourselves. Regardless of our marital status or whether our mothers are still living, we must recognize that we are it. In the most essential sense, we are our beloved; we hold the key to our salvation. But we must walk alongside ourselves each and every step in our journey. We must give ourselves the kind of assurance that we have always yearned for. As we spend time in silence, we will recognize and accept our gifts and uniqueness; as we learn to cope with the ambiguities of life and to live with paradox, as we listen to and trust our inner knowing, as we honor and respect our needs and dreams, as we bring a greater measure of the sacred into our daily lives, we begin to experience ourselves in a new way.

Morgan Farley's poem entitled "The Clearing" speaks eloquently about the process of giving birth to ourselves:

> *I am clearing a space—*
> *here, where the trees stand back.*
> *I am making a circle so open*
> *the moon will fall in love*
> *and stroke these grasses with her silver.*
>
> *I am setting stones in the four directions,*
> *stones that have called my name*
> *from mountaintops and riverbeds, canyons and mesas.*
> *Here I will stand with my hands empty,*
> *mind gaping under the moon.*
>
> *I know there is another way to live.*
> *When I find it, the angels*
> *will cry out in rapture,*
> *each cell of my body*
> *will be a rose, a star.*
>
> *If something seized my life tonight,*
> *if a sudden wind swept through me,*

changing everything,
I would not resist.
I am ready for whatever comes.

But I think it will be
something small, an animal
padding out from the shadows,
or a word spoken so softly
I hear it inside.

It is dark out here, and silent.
The moon is stone.
I am alone with my longing.
Nothing is happening
but the next breath, and the next. . . .

During midlife, we are invited to build a nest, but this time for ourselves. By lavishing some of the sustenance, nurturing, and attention upon ourselves that we would otherwise bestow on a newborn baby, we foster our own wholeness. The emerging self needs to be shown in words and deeds that she is loved, valued, and received. This is the food that will ensure her birth; this is the food that will feed her soul.

Chapter 10

THE RETURN OF THE WILD GIRL

Odder still how possessed I am with the feeling that now, aged 50, I'm just poised to shoot quite free straight & undeflected my bolts whatever they are.

—VIRGINIA WOOLF

Take a moment and think back to when you were between the ages of seven and eleven. What did you love to do? Was it acting in a school play? Was it taking ballet or art classes? Did you spend hours experimenting with your junior chemistry set, collecting stamps, or playing baseball? What happened to that passion? Where did it go? If you're like many of the women I spoke with, most likely it was pruned back as you tried to fit into the culturally prescribed uniform of femininity. Well, now is the time to reclaim our "wild girl" self—to restore her to her rightful place in our lives.

In her book *New Passages*, Gail Sheehy coined the term *wild girl* to describe the enthusiastic, confident, androgynous girl we left behind on the shores of adolescence. I realize that some of you, because of difficult family situations, don't have any recollection of this free-spirited girl. If this is true, I want to reassure you that although you may have no memory of her, she's in there. It may be that she expressed herself through fantasies of being an actress, detective, pilot, teacher, doctor or through characters in books. But even if she was buried beneath the weight of trying childhood circumstances, she's there just waiting for you to make it safe for her to reenter your life. The ponytailed girl in torn blue jeans and plaid shirt can now reappear, if we let her. This is yet another of the essential tasks—or should I say joys?—of midlife.

I know we talked about the virtues of being a bad girl in an earlier chapter. Well, the wild girl is her first cousin. She, too, is tired of being nice. Yet there is a notable difference between the two. The bad girl is a part of our shadow: She represents the darker, selfish, assertive, competitive aspects of our personality. The bad girl is savvy, while the wild girl has a prepubescent purity and genuineness. The bad girl is calculating, measuring the effect of her words and actions, while the wild girl speaks freely, relies on her instincts, and lives in the moment. The bad girl is very much aware of her sexuality and its power, while the wild girl is innocent, unencumbered. She's not yet concerned with being "feminine"; she's just fully and unabashedly herself. The wild girl thinks she can do and accomplish anything. She's filled with a sense of wonder. She's ready to have fun. Sounds like someone you'd like to know, doesn't she? Our wild girl holds our vitality and enthusiasm. She's the one who will keep us young at heart, which is where it counts.

Dreaming Your Dream

We've all had experiences when we were involved in an activity where time passed without our ever having noticed. What were the activities you loved as a girl or as a young woman? Remember the young woman who was fraught with idealism, who wanted to change the world, who took grand risks both in love and in career before she became far too sensible? Where did she go? What did you lay upon the altar of self-sacrifice and offer up to the god of conformity?

It's not just that each of us lost track of our free-spirited self but that there was pressure both from within our families and from society to erase her. In many instances, our wild girl was seen as a threat. For many of us, there was simply no room for her. Our enthusiasm and self-confidence often reminded our mothers of what they had been forced to sacrifice or abandon. While there were exceptions, by and large they believed that the way to ensure their daughters' happiness and security was to teach us to conform—to be "feminine." The societal pressure made it—and unfortunately continues to make it—difficult for the wild girl to remain a vibrant part of a girl's self-image.

In my seminars, I often ask women to consider a question that was first posed by writer Joanna Macy: "What was your dream before you stopped dreaming?" I reassure them that they're under no obligation to follow through with what they say. Inevitably, though, once the women identify what they've lost, they can't wait to integrate it into their lives. Then I ask them to imagine what they would do if money wasn't a concern. I encourage the women to let their imagination run free. This provides a blueprint for recovering the passionate self. In fact, Passionate is our wild girl's middle name. Everything she did was done with intensity, whether it was riding her bike, studying a geode from her mineral collection, or practicing for the school play. She brought her whole self to the task. She had an insatiable curiosity and desire to explore the world.

When you were a girl, did you ever sit in your backyard on a warm summer's night and wonder what made the fireflies twinkle? Did you ever lie on your back and make imaginary creatures out of passing clouds? Were you ever intrigued by how magnets could attract a pile of iron filings or how combining red and blue paint made the color purple? Remember that sense of wonder you felt as a child? Remember the feeling that you wanted to know and do everything? Remember when you could? Well, those feelings are just waiting to be rekindled.

If you need a little inspiration, take yourself where there are children playing. Watch how they peer into a mud puddle in astonishment or hang upside down on the monkey bars, amazed at their new perspective on the world. As you observe these children, allow yourself to remember the delight that is possible when you revive your childhood sense of curiosity.

Ask yourself, What do I crave? For those of us who were once pregnant, we'll remember those cravings. While I'm not talking about food here, the urgency is exactly the same. What is your wild girl calling you to do? You may

hunger to swim naked in a cool mountain lake, to eat a
piece of ripe fruit with your hands, to take swing-dance
lessons. Our cravings can take many forms. They can
range from simple pleasures to the longing for adventure.

The Emergence of New Priorities

Ruth, a woman in her early fifties, came to see me after
having attended one of my seminars. A strategic planner
and city councilwoman, she strode into my office and sat
on the edge of the couch. As she began to talk, she waved
her hands to punctuate her speech. "I have this high-
powered career and a good marriage, but it's not enough
anymore," she said. "When you talked about the wild girl
during your seminar, it just made me sad. I have a nine-
year-old, and there's a real gift in living with my kid.
Franny's the complete essence of a wild girl. She's totally
uninhibited and self-confident. She was in her first dance
recital on Sunday. She was by far the most elementary stu-
dent of the crop of kids. She was half a beat late, watching the bigger girls to figure out where to go next. It's not
like she stood out because of her ability. But she felt fabu-
lous. She had this marvelous, funny little pixie smile on her
face that said, Aren't I just the greatest. She was totally in
the moment and she was happy.

"One of the way's she's a gift is that I get to see in living color the epitome of female health. She's so unencumbered. But in a few short years, she'll be so burdened.
Right now, it's like living with a five-hundred-watt bulb."
Ruth stopped for a moment as tears welled in her eyes. "I
used to be a lot like Franny."

Over the next several sessions, Ruth and I explored what she had given up. As we talked, years melted away. Her daughter's passion and enthusiasm had brought forgotten memories and unexamined experiences to the surface. Now, Ruth could reclaim aspects of herself she had left behind.

"You know, something you asked me sparked a memory," she told me during one session. "You asked if I liked to do things with my hands. Well, I'd forgotten how much I used to love ceramics. I used to take classes after school when I was in second and third grade. I played the clarinet. I took tennis lessons. But I just stopped. I haven't really thought much about what I enjoy. I think I've been on autopilot for a long time. I got married, had a child, and I've been so caught up in running a household, raising my daughter, and developing my career that I completely forgot about what it is that I like." She paused for a moment. "Where did all that passion go? What happened to me? I feel like I gave up something very precious."

Ruth, like so many young women, had sacrificed gifts and dreams throughout the earlier part of her life. Midlife gives a woman the opportunity to question all that she may have been doing unquestioningly earlier in her life. We often discover that many of the compromises and sacrifices that we've made are no longer fulfilling. They begin to feel forced and confining. It's not uncommon to hear women complain, "Is this all there is? There has to be more to life." And, in fact, there is. But we must reprioritize how we spend our time and use our energy in order to forge a strong connection between what we want and what we actually choose to do.

Reclaiming Our Wild Girl

Ruth came to our next session dressed uncharacteristically in a pair of black cotton pants and a T-shirt. She dropped onto the couch and flashed a sheepish grin. "I've done something I've never done before," she said. "Every summer, we visit my husband's family. There's a cabin on a lake; it's been in his family for three generations. We spend the month of August there. But this summer, I've decided to try something new. I talked with my husband about the possibility of going off by myself for two weeks while he took Franny back east. I'd take that time for myself and then join them for the last part of the vacation. He was fine with it. I realized that I'd never in my life been by myself in a house for more than an afternoon. I'd never lived without parents, children, husband, lover, or somebody in the house."

I asked Ruth what she was going to do.

"I have no plans. I have my books, my music, and a piece of needlepoint that I've been working on. It's going to be a time to rediscover myself, with no one to attend to but me. Aren't you jealous?"

"Sounds wonderful," I replied. Ruth and I made an appointment for early September.

When she came to the session, there was a brightness in her eyes and an ease I'd never seen. She was carrying a large canvas bag that she carefully placed beside her. Before I could ask how her summer had been, Ruth said, "I had a great time. My time in the mountains was incredible. I hiked every day. I felt like a pioneer. When I was ten, my best friend and I turned a toolshed into a secret clubhouse. We made up and solved mysteries, kind of like

Nancy Drew. There was something about being in the mountains that reminded me of how I felt then. I was free, and I felt like I could accomplish anything."

After a couple of days, Ruth had discovered an art gallery that was offering a class in pottery of the indigenous Americas. She signed up. "I ended up being the only person in the class," Ruth said. "It was great. We went out to the local mountain, and the instructor taught me how to identify clay. I went out and dug my own. I made my own paint from plants and my own brushes and tools. I collected *vaca caca*."

"*Vaca caca?*" I asked.

"Yeah, cow dung," she explained.

"I dug a pit and fired the pots the way an American Indian would have done it." Ruth took a beautiful black gourd-shaped pot from her bag and handed it to me. "This is what I made." It was exquisite.

"The woman who taught the Jazzercise class I went to turned out to be a law professor from the University of Pennsylvania. She invited me to her house and introduced me to her friends. I sat by the stream that ran past my cabin and read, something I couldn't focus on at home. I have to admit, the first day or two I did miss my husband and daughter. But it was also so delicious just to be alone. There was no phone, no distractions. I could just sit and immerse myself in whatever struck me. While I was up there, I realized that I had suffered from a bad case of tunnel vision. Now I'm determined to have the wide-screen view of life. I think I'm finally catching up with myself at fifty-one."

Ruth rediscovered a curiosity and sense of wonder she hadn't felt since she was a girl. The observation she'd

made at our first session that her daughter was "the epitome of female health" was absolutely true. In her book *The
Girl Within*, Emily Hancock writes, "At the buried core of
women's identity is a distinct and vital self first articulated in childhood, a root identity that gets cut off in the
process of growing up female. . . . Women became truly
themselves only when they recaptured the girl they'd
been in the first place—before she got all cluttered up. . . .
The task of a woman's lifetime boils down to reclaiming
the authentic identity she'd embodied as a girl."

While not every woman is going to rediscover her wild
girl in the same way that Ruth did, she's there waiting for
an invitation to come back into your life. For example,
Cynthia, fifty-one, took ballet lessons for the first time
and danced in the local elementary school performance of
The Nutcracker. Jean, forty-eight, discovered she was an
avid skier, even though she hadn't been athletic earlier in
her life. Margaret, fifty-five, remembered her love of
painting and began watercolor classes. Pam, forty, enrolled
in night school at the local college and read the classics.

What these and other women discovered was that the
resources, strengths, passions, and gifts they had earlier in
their lives were still with them. Whatever they now
choose to set their sights on, be it keeping their marriage
alive, taking up skydiving, going back to school, or finally
committing to a church, they often discover their greatest
assets where they left them years ago.

Poet Sharon Olds speaks about the indomitable spirit of
the wild girl in her poem "Time-Travel":

> *By the shore of the lake there is a girl*
> *twelve years old, watching the water*

fold and disappear. I walk up behind her,
I touch her shoulder, she turns her head—
I see my face. She looks through me
up at the house. This is the one I have
come for. . . . She does not know
any of this will ever stop.
She does not know she is the one
survivor.

Our wild girl must become an essential part of our new adult identity. She's crucial to our becoming whole. The good news is that at midlife, as we step free of society's definition of women as sex objects and childbearers, we can return to a time in our lives when we experienced a greater balance between our masculine and feminine sides. We once again can become more androgynous—the girl who was free to pursue her dreams unencumbered by the limitations of gender. We return to the time when we had our own sense of power, when we focused on exploring the world, our interests and capabilities.

Mild-mannered Businesswoman by Day, Wild Woman by Night

Angela, forty-nine, with a round, full face and reddish brown shoulder-length hair, answered the door. She showed me into a room with a long wooden table. It was covered with neatly piled stacks of papers from a project she had just completed. She's the owner and director of a company that develops low-income housing in urban centers. Angela's on the board of two prominent women's organizations as well as being a member of the steering committee of her daughter's alma mater. You can imagine my surprise when she began to tell me about the middle-of-the-night escapades of her alter ego.

"I think things really started to open up for me right after my divorce," she began. "I saw how destructive it was to spend your life trying to please others. You don't become who you are. It's been a hard lesson for me to learn and one that hasn't been learned quickly. But one of my first breakthroughs was when I decided to do the guerrilla poster campaign about the gag rule."

"Guerrilla postering?" I asked.

"When Bush instituted the executive order that said that federally funded family-planning clinics couldn't give any information to women who came to them about an abortion, I was infuriated," she explained. "It was known as the 'gag rule.' An artist here in L.A., Robbie Conal, developed a 'Gag Me' poster with a picture of Chief Justice William Rehnquist. It said 'Gag Me with a Coat Hanger.'

"I felt a little nervous about putting up posters all over town. It was something I would've never imagined before. It was stepping way out beyond the bounds of propriety. Let me tell you, there were plenty of people who didn't think I should do it. In part because that poster was way too controversial and strong. But I couldn't believe how much I loved doing this. I hadn't had this much fun since I was a girl. It felt like we were being naughty, but not really. You meet the most amazing people—older women, young women."

"What do you do?" I asked, ready to sign up for their next escapade.

"Well, we usually gather at ten-thirty or eleven at night

in an abandoned storefront for a pep talk from Robbie," she said. "He talks about the poster and why he did it. He reminds us about the rules of guerrilla postering. If a police officer tells you to do something, always do it. Then wait five minutes and go back and put the poster up.

"You generally go two or three to a car. One person drives, one gets the poster, and the other puts the glue up wherever we're going to hang it. It could be a construction site. But the best places are signal boxes. You slather the surface with gooey wallpaper paste. Meanwhile, you're looking around to see if there are any police in sight. Sometimes we're quite creative and put two or three posters in a row. We drive around the streets of L.A. at night for about two hours, searching for good spots."

I said, "It sounds like you've done this more than once."

"Oh yes," she responded. "I'm a regular guerrilla girl now."

I told her that I had this image of her, respected businesswoman by day and guerilla posteress by night. We howled with laughter.

"It's true," she said. "I have to admit, it's pretty out of character. But if I'd just gone about doing what I normally do and being nice, I'd never have had this great experience or met these incredible people. I came to discover a whole new sense of freedom. It wasn't about pleasing everyone anymore. Sure, I still feel like I have to maintain important relationships, but doing the postering has given me a lot more permission. I realized that if you do what you believe in, in spite of your discomfort, you project more good into the world, more that's positive and powerful, because it comes from your true beliefs and feelings. Since the start of my postering career, I've branched out and done other things I never would've considered doing before. It's been like discovering buried treasure."

In reclaiming our wild girl, we once again reinstate ourselves as the subjects of our own lives. As strange as it may seem, reconnecting with one's wild self is essential to achieving genuine maturity. Women in our culture, even those of us who were fortunate enough to have grown up with the benefit of feminism, were taught to be polite, proper. Wild was expected of boys, but not for us.

In *Funk & Wagnalls Standard Handbook,* the following antonyms are listed for *wild*: *calm, bland, composed, sedate, serene.* In other words, stifle yourself. *Wild* is defined as "deviating from the intended or expected course"; "unruly, uncivilized"; "without regulation or control." Heaven forbid.

Think for a moment about what might have happened had girls been allowed, let alone encouraged, to follow their wild nature. How different our lives might have been. We would have freely expressed our thoughts, feelings, needs. We would've remained connected to our power and knowing. We would've honored our bodies as the temple of our spirits. We would've pursued our dreams. We would've defined what being feminine meant for ourselves. We would've rejected society's definition of beauty and developed our own. We would've demanded greater equality in our relationships from the outset. And above all, we would have trusted ourselves.

Many of us used to think that maturity meant becoming a stuffy old woman who wears her hair in a bun and has a stern look on her face. But maturity isn't something we arrive at simply because we've reached a certain age. The prerequisite for graduating to this stage of development is the integration of the various parts of one's personality. It requires the synthesis of responsibility and playfulness, complexity and simplicity. It means being filled with wonder while not being naïve. It requires flexibility without compromising our values. As the philosopher Frederick Nietzsche once wrote, "Maturity means acquiring the seriousness one had as a child at play." In retrieving our wild girl, we recover our spontaneity, our capacity for joy, the courage to break the rules. Our wild girl holds the possibility of renewal. She embodies our essence. She expands our world.

The Thirst for Adventure

I can't tell you how many women I've talked with spoke about their desire to break the mold—to do something out of character. One woman, who had dreamed of going on an African safari since she had watched *Wild Kingdom* as a girl, saved up her vacation time and went. Another convinced her husband to stay home with their children while she and a friend went to a dude ranch in Montana. Still another woman and her best friend walked a portion of the Pacific Rim Trail. I could go on recounting these women's escapades. Although they vary dramatically from the exotic to the risky, from the culturally informative to the relaxing, what they all had in common was that they afforded these women an expanded sense of themselves. Our destination isn't as important as allowing ourselves to step outside the well-worn paths of our everyday lives.

In 1996, my daughter, Ama, was doing research in Chiapas, Mexico, for her college thesis. She'd developed a curriculum for a community school in a remote village. Toward the end of her stay, she invited me to join her. She wanted to show me the village where she had worked and introduce me to her friends.

I met Ama in the city. We left the next morning in the dark, changing buses to avoid an immigration checkpoint and military installation. A slight man wearing a cowboy hat met us in the town square. Raul was going to guide us on the three-hour trip up the mountain. At the edge of town, two mules were tied to a tree. I climbed onto one and Raul handed me the lead rope and a switch. Let me tell you, I haven't been on a horse since I was eleven, and that was at a proper English riding stable, jodhpurs and all.

We walked through the jungle, with trees filled with bromeliads covering their branches, past vistas of steep, lush mountains planted with coffee, corn, and bananas. The path dropped steeply down to a river, and I could feel my legs straining as the mule picked its way over boulders. I felt like I'd been transported onto the set of an adventure movie. When I mentioned this to my daughter, she christened me "Indiana Marston." When we finally reached the village, children came running, chanting, "Ama, Ama." People seemed amazed that she had brought her mother to their village. Without ever having said as much I knew we were in a Zapatista community.

We were told that there was going to be a procession for the Virgin of Guadalupe, the patron saint of Mexico, at five o'clock the next morning. Ama and I were awakened by roosters and squealing pigs. As the sky began to brighten, women gathered in the village square, wearing their traditional dress, carrying bougainvilleas, marigolds, and hibiscus flowers. As we prepared to walk to the church, Yasidro, one of the teachers, asked Ama and me if we would carry the plaque with the Virgin of Guadalupe.

The women formed two lines behind us. Two older women draped in black shawls walked beside us, carrying bowls filled with hot coals and burning pine pitch. As we entered the church, sun streamed through open windows made of rough-hewn planks. Chills ran through my body and tears filled my eyes.

We walked the plaque to the makeshift altar and handed it to the priest. The women crowded in around us, while the men filed into the opposite side of the church. As the air filled with the fragrant smoke, prayers were said in Tzotzil, their Mayan language. I had no idea of what was being said, but as I stood among these women, I felt surprisingly at home. I thought about how rich these people were, despite their meager surroundings. Their commitment to family and friends, their connection to the natural world, their sense of community are all values that I cherish. Although we were from different cultures, we shared an unspoken bond.

When the service ended, we were invited to a breakfast of tortillas, beans, and lemongrass tea. We then said our good-byes and began the arduous trip back down the mountain. My sense of myself and the planet were forever altered. To this day, I keep on my bulletin board a photograph of my daughter and me carrying the Virgin of Guadalupe. It reminds me of what's possible when we're willing to risk; it reminds me of the incredible diversity of our world; it reminds me of all the adventures yet to come.

What expeditions have you longed to take? What adventures were abandoned either because of responsibilities or financial concerns? Is there someplace you've always dreamed of going but, for whatever reason, never did? As Joanna Macy asked, was there a dream you once had that you abandoned? Did you want to go to Giverny and walk through the gardens where Monet painted his famous water lilies? Did you want to explore the Grand Canyon? Have you always longed to see the temples of Angkor Wat? While these are pretty exotic-sounding trips, an adventure doesn't necessarily require that we travel far from home or even that we spend money. It simply means that we do something we don't ordinarily do. You can start small with an afternoon escapade, a daylong or weekend outing. And for goodness sake, let yourself fantasize. Wherever it is, start planning and make your dream a reality.

Take Your Passion and Make It Happen

I know that when most of us think about passion, we immediately imagine some hot young lover whisking us away to a tropical island paradise, ripping our clothes off, and making mad, passionate love to us until we have to beg him to stop. Nothing wrong with that, but that's just one facet of this evocative word's meaning. We all remember when we allowed ourselves to be swept away by sexual ardor to the point where little, if anything, else mattered. I know, it was fun, but I'll wager that few of you'd want to go back there.

I'm not talking about the red-hot abandon that inevitably sent us on a tumultuous roller-coaster ride that left us exhausted and spent, but, rather, an authentic pas-

sion that's more like a slow, sustained burn that will ener-
gize our lives. Authentic passion is the spark that we feel
when we've found our true expression, be it trying out an
exotic new recipe, breaking track on freshly fallen snow,
spearheading a campaign against drunk driving, playing
with a grandchild, getting covered in clay while throwing
a pot, raising money to end world hunger, discovering hidden treasure in a secondhand store. It doesn't matter what
it is, as long as you take your passion and make it happen.

What does having passion in your life mean to you? Obviously, each of us must discover this for herself. But if
we're going to remain vital and continue to kick ass—and
I know you intend to—we need a healthy dose of passion
coursing through our veins. We must live our lives fully.

"Several months ago, a friend who is an artist asked if
I'd take a weekend class called Welding for Women,"
Peggy, a fifty-two-year-old financial planner, said. "I'd
never done anything like it before, but I thought it might
be fun. The first day, I was completely intimidated by the
equipment, especially the torches. We had to wear a hel-
met with a small window of tinted glass that we would flip
down over our faces to protect our eyes. This made it difficult to see what we were doing.

"We collected scraps from the yard and practiced tack-
ing pieces together. By the second day, look out. I was into
it. Once I got the hang of using the torches, I loved the
fire. I loved using the grinder, where sparks flew as I bur-
nished and ground pieces of steel, and the hammers,
where I could pound molten metal into different shapes.
I became fire woman. It was so much fun. Who'd have
ever thought of such a thing? But it felt so great to play. I
felt like a kid who had just learned to ride a bike. I re-

turned home from the weekend with a renewed sense of
energy and aliveness. Am I going to give up my day job to
become a welder? Not anytime soon. But it made me realize how wonderful it is to do things that are totally out
of the ordinary."

Come on, baby, light your fire. What do you need to ig-
nite the passion in your life, to bring back that childlike
sense of wonder? Is it a set of pastel crayons, a new pair of
running shoes, a clipboard and a stack of pledge forms, a
copper-bottomed pot? Whatever it is, get it. Indulge yourself. We need to prime our creative pump. This is especially important for those of us whose wild girl never had
a chance to express herself fully as a child.

As you begin to honor your wild self, she'll gain
strength. But you must promise that you'll never again ignore or betray her. This is essential. She must know that
you will acknowledge and honor her. No, I'm not suggesting that you indulge your every whim, but, rather, that you
create space in your life for greater self-expression, fun,
and creativity. If you're not living a passionate life, what
are you waiting for? As novelist Nikos Kazantzakis wrote,
"Leave nothing for death to take, nothing but a few
bones."

Chapter 11

THE GIFTS OF MIDLIFE

And the day came when the risk to remain in the bud was
more painful than the risk it took to bloom.

—ANAÏS NIN

I imagine that before you began reading this book many
of you would have considered the word *gifts* linked with
midlife a contradiction in terms. It certainly is as far as
our society is concerned. I hope by now, though, you appreciate the immense opportunities this time has to
offer. Yes, I know we're rapidly becoming the "older generation." Yes, I know we're no longer the target audience
for television shows or commercials. Yes, I know our
music's been categorized as "oldies," our styles as
"retro." Yes, I know society no longer considers us babes.
Yet midlife itself is an extraordinary gift. Just in case
there are any lingering doubts, let me remind you—let

me count the ways that this midlife journey can enrich and enliven us.

Midlife offers us an unusual opportunity to look back over our lives as well as to look forward. It provides us with a chance for reevaluation and, if need be, for course corrections. Midlife allows us to redefine our attractiveness based on our own preferences, rather than on culturally prescribed standards. It gives us an opportunity to harvest the wisdom, power, and strength we've acquired during the first half of our lives. Midlife calls upon us to recognize our complexity and to integrate the neglected aspects of our personality in order to become whole. It allows us to become more understanding and accepting of ourselves. At midlife, we discover a more flexible, confident self and finally become comfortable in our own skin. During this time, our spirituality takes on a deeper dimension as we live our values hour by hour, day by day. It compels us to live more fully, to seize the moment—to realize our dreams.

Here are some of the many benefits that women have received during this passage: "There's a oneness with humanity that I feel as I get older. There are fewer differences between people than there are similarities. I can now bring this understanding into my relationships." "I don't care what people think of me anymore. I feel like I'm my own person. I do what I know is right." "It's great to be a woman. I'm no longer so caught up in society's expectations of how women are supposed to be. I'm less concerned about looking a certain way and am more interested in suiting myself." "I've developed a keen BS detector. I feel a new comfort in being able to say no and making choices about how I want to spend my time." "When I was younger, I wanted to fit in. I've retired the need to prove myself. Now my quirkiness has become what I like best about myself. I feel a freedom to be more unconventional. That's a wonderful gift." "I've finally discovered how to make myself happy and that it really is up to me." "The older I get, the more I have to give. That's a gift for me that becomes a gift for others."

These are just some of the legacies the women I spoke with expressed. Yet along with these gifts comes a certain amount of responsibility.

At midlife, we have the rare opportunity to own what we know, what we've experienced, what we've accomplished. We also have a chance to become more connected with our passion, vitality, wisdom, strength—the fullness of who we are. It's also our chance to give something back to the world. At midlife, we are called to share all that we've reaped from these years of living, especially from this passage. It's time to make a meaningful contribution, not from a sense of obligation, but from a place of fullness.

I know some of you must be thinking, Why is she talking about giving when that's what we've done all our adult lives? But once we can trust that we'll attend to our own needs and dreams, then we can become a catalyst for positive change. Then we can devote some of our energy to mothering the larger family. It's what Erik Erikson described as "generativity"—the desire to leave a legacy, to share the gifts, talents, and knowledge we've accumulated during the first half of our lives.

I know, it's kind of amazing to think that we're actually in a position of being an elder, someone whom other people look to for guidance. I admit, it takes a bit of getting used to. But we're there. And if the truth be known, it feels pretty wonderful. To think that all of our hard work and determination has not only paid off for us but has a larger purpose. I don't know about you, but I'm starting to see that this aging thing definitely has its pluses.

In most cultures, becoming an elder bestows a certain amount of authority. Elders are considered respected members of the community. The wisdom that can only be obtained from life experience is highly valued. In fact, in societies where there is less of a fixation on youth, elders are often revered.

Me, a Role Model!

We all grew up with women we admired—Eleanor Roosevelt, Margaret Mead, Katharine Hepburn, Rosa Parks, Amelia Earhart, Rachel Carson—older women, women of our mothers' generation whom we looked up to. Of course, there were also women closer to home whom we wanted to emulate. We used these women to define ourselves. They would mirror who we wanted to be, what we wanted to learn, what we dreamed of accomplishing. We would imitate them—try out different attributes—and, little by little, we developed many of the characteristics we admired.

We all know women in their seventies and eighties who play tennis, are docents at museums, volunteer for charities, and continue to travel the world. These women are our inspirations. They point the way to what's possible. As we once again move into uncharted territory, we look to these older women—women who are living full, vibrant lives—as role models as we become role models ourselves. Without having realized it, we've become role models, certainly for our own children, but for others, as well.

A few months ago, my twenty-six-year-old daughter had

gone to a mechanic to have the bumper replaced on her 1984 Honda. When she received the bill, it was more than double what had been agreed upon. When she confronted the man, he made the excuse that there had been additional labor involved, but he said he couldn't reach her to discuss it. When she called me, she was furious. "Mom," she said, "he never would've done this if I were a man. I may look innocent and easygoing, but I'm not. I have Grandma's dragon genes. He's messing with the wrong girl." I encouraged her to hold him to the agreed-upon price.

When I hung up the phone, not only did I feel a sense of pride for my daughter but I realized that all my years of donning my warrior outfit had made an impression on her. It also occurred to me that this was part of the legacy that I had inherited from my mother and had now passed on to my own daughter. As Eleanor Roosevelt said, "The influence you exert is through your own life and what you become yourself."

One of the many blessings of midlife is the ability to share our legacy with generations of younger women. We stand on the shoulders of the women who have gone before us—our mothers, grandmothers, great-grandmothers, our sisters, teachers, aunts. There's a joy and privilege in being able to offer the countless women who will follow in our footsteps our knowledge and wisdom.

Angela, the forty-nine-year-old urban planner who had done the guerrilla postering, said, "I have a room downstairs in my house, and for the last four or five years I've had various women in their twenties living with me, not my children. I love those relationships. I have such respect for these young women. Who they are and what they want to accomplish are really inspiring. They're very nurturing for me. Not only do I get a sense of how twenty-year-olds are thinking but I have an opportunity to help them get some perspective on situations they face at work or in their own crises of confidence.

"Most of my life, I didn't feel that I had a lot to offer. But in the past few years, especially since I've had these girls staying with me, that's changed. I'm discovering that I do, in fact, have a great deal to offer. It's a little intimidating. It means I have to take myself more seriously. It means I have to respect myself, my intellect, and the knowledge I've gained through the years.

"These young women come to me with questions about their lives. It's great to be able to share my own experiences, not that theirs are going to be the same. It reminds me of all that I've learned."

The way we live our lives, especially how we embrace this process of aging, is crucial. We're showing the younger generation how to grow older without getting old—what aging can look like at its fullest.

I Am She as You Are She as You Are Me and We Are All Together

One of the great gifts of midlife is having a deeper sense of ourselves. This invariably allows us to be more understanding and accepting of others. That's the extraordinary next step—we have an opportunity to see beyond ourselves. We have a chance to recognize and honor the equality of all beings. We can now acknowledge that we are related to everything and everyone. Despite our differences in race, sexual preference, socioeconomic status, ethnicity, age, we're essentially the same. We have the same hopes, fears, struggles, needs, and joys. We all share the desire to attain happiness and avoid suffering.

With this realization, we can begin to experience the world as an extension of ourselves. In Alice Walker's novel *The Color Purple*, the character Celie expressed this idea of interdependence: "One day when I was sitting quiet and feeling like a motherless child, which I was, it come to me: that feeling of being part of everything, not separate at all. I knew that if I cut a tree, my arm would bleed." Interconnectedness emerges from a deep respect for ourselves and others. One of the tasks of midlife is to extend love, compassion, and forgiveness into the world. This notion is the foundation of every world religion. Now, more than ever, it also becomes a dynamic principle in our own lives. As we have been able to embrace our own imperfections, the ways in which we've disappointed and failed ourselves, we discover greater understanding and self-acceptance. The peace and healing we want to bring into the world begins with us. When we recognize that we are just as capable of causing hurt, that we have spoken out in anger, made as many mistakes as the next person, we can begin to become more forgiving of others. Writer Christina Baldwin writes, "Forgiveness is the act of admitting we are like other people."

Admit it, we all walk around judging and criticizing others. It's a way to keep us from having to admit that we are just as imperfect and fallible as the woman who drags her child through the supermarket, as the man who rarely makes it home in time to have dinner with his family, or as the woman who stays with a man who's obviously neglectful. I'm as guilty of being critical as the next gal. But pretending that we're somehow better than the next person only serves to enforce our separateness.

We've all been angry at our parents, siblings, spouses, exes, you name it. But let's face it: We're not going to make them redo the past. It's simply not going to happen. We have a choice. We can either hold on to our anger and allow it to poison our lives or we can find a way to let go of our old grudges. It seems like a no-brainer, but, as we all know, it's no small feat to forgive those who have hurt us. Yet when we can put ourselves in their shoes and try to understand the desperation, fear, or ignorance that was the origin of their actions—when we truthfully consider whether we could have done or have done something similar—it becomes somewhat easier.

When we refuse to forgive, not only does our resentment impede our moving fully into the second half of our lives but we're pretending that we aren't as flawed as the rest of humanity. By now, we should know better. Forgiveness insists that we admit that we're just like every other human being who's doing the best they can with what they presently know. Forgiveness requires us to open our hearts to the suffering of others.

In her poem "The Weighing," Jane Hirshfield speaks of the power of forgiveness:

> *The heart's reasons*
> *seen clearly,*
> *even the hardest*
> *will carry*
> *its whip-marks and sadness*
> *and must be forgiven.*

As the drought-starved
eland forgives
the drought-starved lion
who finally takes her,
enters willingly then
the life she cannot refuse,
and is lion, is fed,
and does not remember the other.

So few grains of happiness
measured against all the dark
and still the scales balance.

The world asks of us
only the strength we have and we give it.
Then it asks more, and we give it.

Compassion and forgiveness allow us to rejoin the larger community. However, compassion doesn't require that we ignore ourselves. It simply means that we allow ourselves to experience an intimate connection with another person, to be able genuinely to know their suffering. No matter what the situation, compassion is the appropriate response. If we can see the person's actions, no matter how hurtful, as a cry for healing, we're more likely to be able to extend our empathy. This is a tall order, especially when the other person is acting in a way that causes pain to you or someone you love. But the question is, Can we stretch ourselves to be more than we thought we could be? Can we find a greater generosity than we thought we were capable of? And as challenging as *this* may sound, compassion isn't enough. We must take action. We must put our caring and concern into practice.

Sharing the Wealth

Caring is instinctive. A child is lost; we help her find her parents. Someone trips; we reflexively reach out to break his fall. A coworker's car won't start; we offer her a ride home. It's a natural part of being human. We live; therefore, we help. Helping occurs because the obstacles that separate us drop away, and so we are, in essence, caring for ourselves. We help because the homeless person begging for food is us. We help because the person on welfare who is worried about feeding her family is us. We help because the gang member defending his turf is us. We help because the child who is abused and needs a safe haven is also us.

Among the questions I ask women in my seminars are: "How can you use your whole self to be of service in the world?" "How can you use the wisdom you have gained from your life experience to better our planet?" "Whom do you feel the most compelled to serve?" Take a moment and consider what it is you truly care about. Is it teen pregnancy? Social justice? The environment? Homelessness? Endangered species? World hunger? Human rights? There's no absence of issues that need your time, energy, and dedication. "In a time lacking in truth and certainty and filled with anguish and despair," writes poet Louise Bogan, "no woman should be shamefaced in attempting to give back to the world, through her work, a portion of its lost heart."

Some women I spoke with felt that what they were able to give wouldn't be enough to make a meaningful contribution. When I heard this, more often than not, it seemed like an excuse not to get involved. For those women who are in doubt, this story's for you.

Author Jack Canfield tells this tale. One day, a woman was walking down a deserted beach in Mexico. As she walked along, she saw another person in the distance. When she got closer, she noticed that the person was picking something up and hurling it over and over into the ocean.

As the woman got closer, she noticed that the person was picking up starfish that had been washed ashore. One at a time, she was throwing them back into the water. The woman was puzzled. She walked up to the person and said, "Good morning. I was wondering what you're doing."

"I'm throwing these starfish back into the sea," the person said. "They've been washed ashore in the low tide. If I don't throw them back, they'll die."

"I understand," the woman said, "but there must be thousands all over the beach. You can't possibly get to all of them. There're simply too many."

The person smiled, bent down, and picked up yet another starfish. As she tossed it back into the sea, she said, "Made a difference to that one."

When a woman asks, "What do I have to give?" my response is, "Everything—everything you've learned and experienced, everything you are. Which is considerable." No, most of us aren't going to become Mother Teresa, devote our lives to service, and move to Calcutta. But that's not what's being asked of us. What we're being called to do is what we can—to make a contribution, no matter how modest.

Giving can take many forms. We can start small by taking supper to a sick friend, writing a letter to the editor, volunteering for a school fund-raiser, helping someone change a flat tire. Perhaps it's as simple as extending common courtesies, making thoughtful gestures, offering words of encouragement to the people we interact with on a daily basis.

In case you need a little inspiration, here are what some of the women I interviewed are doing.

Cordelia, a fifty-seven-year-old artist: "I volunteer one week every summer at a camp for women who are living with HIV and AIDS. They range in age from nineteen to sixty. They're all at different stages of the disease. I run the arts and crafts room. I always have one major project—either mask making or spirit dolls. These women have never been exposed to art. That's what's so incredible. They're like little children learning to create for the first time. They come the first day, and they're scared and vulnerable. They tell me they can't do art. But by the last day, every piece is a masterpiece. Their work is so pure. It comes from the heart.

"Every day in the art room, we laugh together; we cry together; we solve problems together. They're so thrilled with everything they do and they're so proud. I'd started to feel that art had gotten so elitist. This is taking art back out to the people. Working with these women feeds my soul more than anything. It's like nothing I've ever experienced."

Nancy, a forty-five-year-old documentary filmmaker: "We have a bridge on our property that goes over a creek. We discovered that there was a colony of about one thousand bats under the bridge. There's a biologist who's been working on the Bats and Bridges Project. She told us that the colony on our property was the largest in the area. It is especially significant because Public Works was trying to renovate the bridges, and we were worried that they would disturb these historic bat colonies. Unless someone started documenting what was going on, the bridges might be torn down and the habitats destroyed.

"I have two children, thirteen and fifteen. I wanted to promote their sense of civic responsibility. So our family became part of a team of bat counters. The colony at our bridge is a nursery colony. The other two bridges seem to have mostly males. Along with my kids' school, we've helped build bat houses so that when the county actually does the work on these bridges, the bats will hopefully have another place to go. We were actually able to get Public Works to delay their plans and consider what type of precautions they should take in renovating the bridges. Whatever they decide should set a precedent in other communities."

Michele, a fifty-year-old massage therapist: "I was burned-out and was going to Mexico to recharge my battery. Before I left, I started to have dreams about Eastern Europe. Then I got a postcard from a friend who had recently moved to Budapest. Within the same week, I received a letter requesting a massage therapist to go into Bosnia and train doctors. Even *I* couldn't ignore all these signs. I traded in my ticket to Mexico and bought one to Hungary. While I was there, I made a connection to go to the largest refugee camp, which was on the Croatian border.

"When I arrived, the people were cautious. There had been a lot of foreigners who came into the camp, took photographs, wrote stories, and never came through with any help. That, combined with the language barrier, made it difficult. So I decided just to show them what I did. I worked with as many people as I could. By the second day, they gave me free rein to work in the hospital, the nursing home, and with any individual who was interested.

"When I returned home, I realized that this was what I wanted to do. I started an organization called Compassionate Touch. I had no idea of how I was going to fund it; I just knew I had to. I found someone to sponsor me so that I could receive tax-deductible donations. It built from there. I just returned from my fourth trip. This last time, I concentrated on the children. They are the emissaries who can bring touch into their families. I also started a pen-pal project, sharing crafts and letters between the schoolchildren of our two countries. There's so much trauma as a result of the war. I want to help heal some of that through touch."

Audrey, a sixty-year-old retired actress and novelist: "Ten years ago, my mother had put together a book of children's poems about bugs and sea creatures. Her agent had taken it around, but he was unsuccessful. It just sat there for all these years. My mother was an alcoholic, and it was difficult for me to be around her. She had such a volatile personality. In the past few years, she had to go on oxygen, and she stopped getting out of bed. She had always expected me to do something with her book, but I was struggling with my own life.

"A few years ago, I had written a novel and had just gotten the galleys back. It was such a wonderful feeling that I wanted to give my mother the same gift. I called my father and said, 'If I can get Mother's book published, would you pay for it?'

"He said, 'The only thing in my life I regret is not privately publishing your mother's writing.'

"He gave me five thousand dollars, and I went and found a designer. I called my mother's seventy-nine-year-old sister, who is an artist, and asked if she could do the illustrations. Then I realized that you had to have an ISBN and a Library of Congress Number. It turned into a whole involved project. But I never enjoyed anything more. I had this goal of putting my mother's book in her hands Christmas morning. Figuring out what to get my mother for Christmas had always been a whale in my life. It became even more difficult now that she was bedridden. I decided that I was going to give her the gift of herself.

"My first print run was two hundred and fifty copies. I wrote to all my mother's friends and told them I was publishing her book. I sent them the galley and asked each of them to write a little blurb. They all did. The printer sent a copy to me and a copy to my mother. They arrived on Christmas Eve. I was literally over the moon. I've never been so thrilled or so happy as when I held this little book.

"The book was put in my mother's hands Christmas morning. She saw her poetry published. She saw all the endorsements from her friends. We gave thirty-three books to the Memphis library; we gave them to the Memphis Zoo. We sent them off to all my mother's friends. People wrote her thank-you letters and called her to tell her how wonderful they thought the book was. My mother died in August. But she got to live with that success for nine months. It took care of a lot that had been between us. I finally felt as though I had done something right for her. I think she was deeply honored and pleased."

The Blessings of Giving

At midlife, fulfillment occurs from using our gifts to give back to the greater community. As we complete this passage, service becomes an act of gratitude, an expression of our reverence for life. We recognize that we're part of a larger tapestry that must be woven together to strengthen the social fabric of our planet. Get into the habit of helping. Cultivate your natural caring and compassion. Share the wealth of all that you are with the world.

Our impact goes beyond what each of us can contribute as individuals. We live on through our good works, the people we mentor, the programs we create. Making a contribution sets off a chain reaction. Each person we touch passes on the kindness and caring to another person, and in this way, our actions have a ripple effect.

Midlife is truly a chance to make a contribution to our larger family. As you can see from the women in this chapter, we can do this in myriad ways, from broad, sweeping gestures to simple acts of kindness. We give back by our very example. We give back by what we do. We give back by sharing our experiences. In essence, we're becoming living treasures, repositories of knowledge, compassion, encouragement, inspiration.

In a larger sense, our generation has the opportunity to provide the ultimate gift—an entirely new notion of what midlife can be. We are redrawing the blueprints for aging. We're redefining what this time of our lives can be. We're dispelling the fears that midlife is the beginning of the end and, instead, establishing that midlife is a new beginning: a time rich in opportunities, a time to be cherished and savored, a time to be celebrated. Midlife can be—should be—one of the best times of our lives. The choice lies with you. After all, if not now, when?

Epilogue

Not long ago, some friends from Los Angeles came to visit. Whenever I have out-of-town guests, I like to take them on a tour of the city. We were strolling along Canyon Road, the hub of the Santa Fe art scene, wandering in and out of galleries. We entered one, and I was immediately drawn to a painting on the far wall entitled *The Crossing*. The piece was of a lone figure, adrift, on a storm-tossed sea. There was no land in sight, yet she appeared calm, centered, her gaze steadfast. There was something reassuring about the painting. I had never bought any original art, but I knew that I had to have this piece.

When I brought the painting home, I began to think about how simple the image was: a woman in an open boat. She was naked, stripped down to the bare essentials. There was no one to guide her. She was it. She had to make her way on her own. It was exactly how I felt about my life. Yet she seemed unfazed by her circumstance, while I often felt undone. Why? What made this difference? How had she managed this? And more important, how could I?

A few days later, I invited a friend over. She found the painting dark and disturbing. I was surprised. I'd never seen it that way. It had always seemed so hopeful, so full of promise. After she left, I spent hours staring at the piece, as if it held the key to a mystery I was desperately trying to solve. The more I stared, the more I saw. I began to see subtle colors in the sky and a single star I hadn't noticed before. Was the woman using the star to guide her? Was that why she appeared so calm? Could it be that having an unchanging focus could make the difference between chaos and serenity? I realized that I, too, needed to find a constant, a way to steady myself, to not be so blown around by the winds of change.

I began to think about how sailors, when lost at sea, locate Polaris, the North Star, to navigate their way home. When everything else fails, they can chart their course by that enduring light in the night sky.

I started to wonder, What would be my North Star? What could I use to navigate this second half of my life? What could I count on that would be consistent, when everything in my life was in such flux? I knew that I needed a new compass, not one that I held in my hand, but one that resided in my heart.

My old compass had gone haywire from overexposure to the pull of the world. I could no longer rely on it. I needed something that I could count on to keep me true. The more I thought about it, the clearer the answer became. I needed to follow my own North Star—my authentic self. It has been and will forever remain the constant in my life. This would be the beacon that could see me through even the roughest storms. This is what I could depend upon to guide me toward the fulfillment of my dreams.

Yet I knew that it would take more than this realization to keep me on track. I had to find a way to keep this discovery present in my life. The painting became my reference point. I began to ask myself regularly, Is this decision consistent with my deepest self? Will it keep me on course? I incorporated these questions into my daily meditation and prayer, until it became as natural as breathing. I don't mean to imply that I never get thrown by the challenges in my life. Far from it. Yet following my North Star, my truest, most enduring self, has gone a long way toward creating greater peace and clarity in my life.

Through this midlife journey, we have the opportunity to reconnect with our truest, most enduring self. As we emerge from this passage, we experience a more direct connection with our power, strength, and wisdom. We feel an urgency to attend to our unfulfilled needs and longings. We discover a new commitment to nurture our creativity and passion. From this new vantage point, we're able to look back over the patterns of our lives, understand their meaning, and better accept our past and ourselves. Out of this expanded sense of self, we discover a greater contentment, flexibility, vitality, and compassion. Our challenge now is to remain focused on who we truly are, what we believe in, and what we love. As we do, we can chart the course for this next phase of the journey.

Author's Note

Any comments or questions regarding the issues raised in this book will be welcomed.

Please contact Stephanie Marston at:
Post Office Box 31453
Santa Fe, New Mexico 87594-1453
505-989-7596 (phone)
505-989-4486 (fax)

Or at her Web site:
www.stephaniemarston.com

Notes

Chapter 1
THE CALL OF THE AUTHENTIC SELF

15 Research conducted with the alumnae of Mills College: Valory Mitchell and Ravenna Helson, "Women's prime of life: Is it the 50's?" *Psychology of Women Quarterly* 14 (1990):451–470; cited in Linda N. Edelstein, *Art of Midlife* (Westport, Connecticut: Bergin & Garvey, 1999), p. 62.

15 A 1955 *New York Times* article on women college students: Nancy Woloch, *Women and the American Experience* (New York: Alfred A. Knopf, 1984), p. 500.

18 "Part of me is dying": Steven Levine, *Meeting at the Edge* (New York: Doubleday, 1989), p. 106.

19 "Most people prefer": Virginia Satir, *Old Sayings I Just Made Up* (Palo Alto, California: Avanta Network, 1989).

20 "adolescence is a time": Carol Gilligan, Nona P. Lyons, and Trudy J. Hanmer, eds., *Making the Connection: The Relational Worlds of Adolescent Girls at Emma Willard School* (Cambridge, Massachusetts: Harvard University Press, 1990), p. 4.

22 "being my own person": Ravenna Helson and Geraldine Moane, "Personality Change in Women from College to Midlife," *Journal of*

Personality and Social Psychology 53 (1987):181; cited in Edelstein, *The Art of Midlife*, p. 117.

Chapter 2
STRUT YOUR STUFF EVEN IF IT'S SAGGING

30 "A grown woman should not have to masquerade": Germaine Greer, *The Change: Women, Aging and the Menopause* (New York: Fawcett Columbine, 1991), p. 4.

30 Our generation invests more energy, time, and money: Karen Kaigler-Walker, Ph.D, *Positive Aging: Every Woman's Quest for Wisdom and Beauty* (Berkeley: Conair Press, 1997), p. 3.

30 In 1997, we spent $1.3 billion: CBS News report, May 29, 1999.

31 "The attempt to hold on to": Betty Freidan, *The Fountain of Age* (New York: Simon and Schuster, 1993), p. 30.

34 "It's taken me twenty years": Gloria Steinem, *Revolution from Within: A Book of Self-Esteem* (Boston: Little, Brown), p. 227.

34 Plastic surgery is on the rise: *New York Times,* June 21, 1998.

36 "For if youth is linked to beauty": Judith Viorst, *Necessary Losses* (New York: Simon and Schuster, 1986), p. 268.

40 "I realize that I was obviously dealing": Elissa Melamed, *Mirror, Mirror: The Terror of Not Being Young* (New York: Linden Press, 1983), p. 11.

42 "You only begin to discover": V. Tiger and C. Sprauge, eds., *The Critical Essays on Doris Lessing* (Boston: G. K. Hall); cited in Greer, *The Change*, p. 52.

44 "Once past 50": Carolyn Heilbrun, "How Girls Become Wimps," *New York Times Book Review,* October 4, 1992, p. 13. (Heilbrun was reviewing Lyn Mikel Brown and Carol Gilligan's *Meeting at the Crossroads*.)

44 "an interest in her body": Terri Apter, *The Secret Path: Women in the New Midlife* (New York: W. W. Norton and Company), p. 63.

46 There was an article: Warren Hoge, "The Stately 'Calendar Girls' Give Their All, Except Pearls," *New York Times,* September 23, 2000.

51 In 1900, the average woman lived: C. Costello and A. J. Stone, eds., *The American Woman: 1994–95* (New York: W. W. Norton, 1995); cited in Joan Borysenko, Ph.D., *A Woman's Book of Life* (New York: Riverhead Books, 1996), p. 5.

52 Studies show that women who: Barbara A. Brehm, Ed.D., "Exercise Benefits for Midlife Women," *Fitness Management Magazine* (Los Angeles), 15, no. 2:27.

52 In a Harvard study: Judith Reichman, M.D., *I'm Too Young to Get Old* (New York: Random House, 1996), p. 417.

Chapter 3
THE *M* WORD

57 Women's bodies during menopause: Christiane Northrup, M.D., *Women's Bodies, Women's Wisdom* (New York: Bantam Books, 1994), p. 432.

58 With 50 million women currently experiencing menopause: Natalie Angier, *Woman: An Intimate Geography* (Boston: Houghton Mifflin, 1999), p. 207.

59 The average woman completes the transformation: C. Costello and A. J. Stone, eds., *The American Woman: 1994–95* (New York: W. W. Norton, 1995), p. 198.

60 But only 46 percent of postmenopausal women: Angier, *Woman*, pp. 212, 213.

61 Dr. Christiane Northrup notes: ibid., p. 10.

66 "Perhaps one of the rewards of aging": Gloria Steinem, *Revolution from Within* (Boston: Little, Brown, 1992), p. 246.

68 In many traditional societies: Barbara G. Walker, *The Woman's Encyclopedia of Myths and Secrets* (New York: Harper San Francisco, 1983), p. 641.

69 Among the Maori: Allan B. Chinen, *Once Upon a Midlife* (New York: Putnam, 1993), p. 168; cited in Kathleen A. Brehony, *Awakening at Midlife* (New York: Riverhead, 1996), p. 142.

70 The founding fathers of the United States: story from Christiane Northrup's PBS special, *Women's Bodies, Women's Wisdom.*

Chapter 4
SEX, DRUGS, AND MENOPAUSE

78 Approximately 70 percent of women: AARP/*Modern Maturity* Sexuality Study, reported in *Modern Maturity,* September–October 1999, p. 41.

78 "Because our society views menopause": Christiane Northrup, *Women's Bodies, Women's Wisdom* (New York: Bantam Books, 1994), p. 457.

79 "At least 50 percent of menopausal women": J. Pfenninger, "Sex and the Maturing Female," *Mature Health* (January–February 1987), pp. 12–13; William Masters and Virginia Johnson, *Human Sexual Response* (Boston: Little, Brown, 1966), pp. 117, 238.

79 "The women's capacity for orgasm": William H. Masters et al., *Heterosexuality* (New York: HarperCollins, 1994), p. 470, citing B. D. Starr and M. B. Weiner, *The Starr-Weiner Report on Sex and Sexuality in the Mature Years* (New York: Stein and Day, 1981).

Chapter 5
DON'T WANT NOTHIN' BUT THE REAL THING, BABY

95 "ethics of care": Carol Gilligan, *In a Different Voice: The Psychological Theory and Women's Development* (Cambridge, Massachusetts: Harvard University Press, 1982), pp. 62–63.

104 "The old conspiracies are abandoned": Roger L. Gould, M.D., *Transformations: Growth and Change in Adult Life* (New York: Simon and Schuster, 1978), p. 291.

109 "In a growing relationship": Anne Morrow Lindbergh, *Gifts from the Sea* (New York: Pantheon, 1975), pp. 69–70.

Chapter 6

GROWING UP ISN'T FOR SISSIES

126 "Our subjective experience": Roger Gould, "Transformational Tasks in Adulthood," in Stanley Greenspan and George Pollack, eds., *The Course of Life*, vol. 3. (Madison, Connecticut: International University Press, 1989), p. 58.

130 "Life as we have known it is over": Marion Woodman, *The Pregnant Virgin* (Toronto: Inner City Books, 1985), p. 7.

137 "A world that can be explained": Albert Camus, *The Myth of Sisyphus* (New York: Vintage Books, 1959), p. 5.

139 "When you try to stay on the surface": Alan W. Watts, *The Wisdom of Insecurity* (New York: Vintage Books, 1951), p. 9.

Chapter 7

GHOSTS IN THE DARKNESS

153 "Look for your other half": Antonio Machado, Robert Bly, Translator, *Times Alone: Selected Poems of Antonio Machado* (Middletown, Connecticut: Wesleyan University Press, 1983), p. 147.

170 "Power is the ability": Carolyn Heilbrun, *Writing a Woman's Life* (New York: Ballantine Books, 1988), p. 18.

Chapter 8
We All Need Somebody to Lean On

173 "A friend is someone you can call": Anne Beatts, *Vogue*, August 1981, cited in Barbara Alpert, *The Love of Friends: A Celebration of Women's Friendships* (New York: Berkley Books, 1997).

178 "The first duty of love is to listen": Martin Buber, *I and Thou* (New York: Charles Scribner's Sons, 1970).

185 "In times of trouble": Maya Angelou quoted in Sherry Ruth Anderson and Patricia Hopkins, *The Feminine Face of God* (New York: Bantam Books, 1991), p. 212.

193 "An honorable human relationship": Adrienne Rich, *On Lies, Secrets, and Silence: Selected Prose 1966–1978* (New York: W. W. Norton, 1979), p. 188.

Chapter 9
Giving Birth to Ourselves

197 Famous Indian story: cited in James W. Jones, *In the Middle of This Road We Call Our Life* (San Francisco: Harper San Francisco, 1995), p. 25.

203 "Here I am alone": May Sarton, *Journal of a Solitude* (New York: W. W. Norton, 1973), p. 11.

205 "I am not I": *Federico G. Lorca and Juan R. Jiménez: Selected Poems*, ed. and trans. Robert Bly (Boston: Beacon Press, 1973), p. 77.

211 "This is an absolute necessity": Joseph Campbell, *The Power of Myth* (Garden City, New York: Doubleday, 1988).

215 In a Hasidic tale: Martin Buber, *Tales of Hasidim: The Later Masters* (New York: Schoken Books, 1948), p. 251.

217 "I am clearing a space": Morgan Farley, "The Clearing," reprinted with permission of the author.

Chapter 10
THE RETURN OF THE WILD GIRL

227 "At the buried core": Emily Hancock, *The Girl Within* (New York: Fawcett Columbine, 1989), pp. 3–4.

227 "By the shore of the lake": Sharon Olds, "Time-Travel," *Satan Says* (Pittsburgh: University of Pittsburgh Press, 1980), pp. 61–62.

Chapter 11
THE GIFTS OF MIDLIFE

244 "One day when I was sitting quiet": Alice Walker, *The Color Purple* (New York: Harcourt Brace, 1992), p. 167.

244 "Forgiveness is the act": Christina Baldwin, *Life's Companion: Journal Writing as a Spiritual Quest* (New York: Bantam Books, 1991).

245 "The heart's reasons": Jane Hirshfield, *October Palace Poems* (New York: HarperPerennial, 1994), p. 79.

248 Author Jack Canfield tells: Jack Canfield, *Chicken Soup for the Soul* (Deerfield, Florida: Health Communications, 1983), pp. 22–23.

Index